CAMBRIDGE LIBRARY COLLECTION

Books of enduring scholarly value

History

The books reissued in this series include accounts of historical events and movements by eye-witnesses and contemporaries, as well as landmark studies that assembled significant source materials or developed new historiographical methods. The series includes work in social, political and military history on a wide range of periods and regions, giving modern scholars ready access to influential publications of the past.

Knocking About in New Zealand

Little is known about Charles L. Money, who sailed in 1861 from Gravesend to New Zealand, where, as he recounts in this volume, he spent the next seven years, working as a gold prospector, a surveyor, a sheep hand, a baker's boy, and a log splitter. He also spent periods in the military, serving in McDonnell's campaign against the Maori in the second Taranaki war (1863–6), which was instrumental in establishing colonial control of the area, and participating in the notorious Pokaikai raid, an eyewitness account of which is included in the book. Money also, pragmatically, worked with, and occasionally for, the Maori. His narrative provides source material for social tensions in this formative period of New Zealand history, as well as giving a vivid picture of the hardships of emigrant life. It was published in 1871 by Samuel Mullen, the owner of the first literary library and bookshop in Australia.

Cambridge University Press has long been a pioneer in the reissuing of out-of-print titles from its own backlist, producing digital reprints of books that are still sought after by scholars and students but could not be reprinted economically using traditional technology. The Cambridge Library Collection extends this activity to a wider range of books which are still of importance to researchers and professionals, either for the source material they contain, or as landmarks in the history of their academic discipline.

Drawing from the world-renowned collections in the Cambridge University Library, and guided by the advice of experts in each subject area, Cambridge University Press is using state-of-the-art scanning machines in its own Printing House to capture the content of each book selected for inclusion. The files are processed to give a consistently clear, crisp image, and the books finished to the high quality standard for which the Press is recognised around the world. The latest print-on-demand technology ensures that the books will remain available indefinitely, and that orders for single or multiple copies can quickly be supplied.

The Cambridge Library Collection will bring back to life books of enduring scholarly value (including out-of-copyright works originally issued by other publishers) across a wide range of disciplines in the humanities and social sciences and in science and technology.

Knocking About in New Zealand

CHARLES L. MONEY

CAMBRIDGE
UNIVERSITY PRESS

CAMBRIDGE UNIVERSITY PRESS

Cambridge, New York, Melbourne, Madrid, Cape Town,
Singapore, São Paolo, Delhi, Tokyo, Mexico City

Published in the United States of America by Cambridge University Press, New York

www.cambridge.org
Information on this title: www.cambridge.org/9781108039499

© in this compilation Cambridge University Press 2012

This edition first published 1871
This digitally printed version 2012

ISBN 978-1-108-03949-9 Paperback

KNOCKING ABOUT

IN

NEW ZEALAND.

BY

CHARLES L. MONEY.

Melbourne:

SAMUEL MULLEN, 55 COLLINS STREET EAST.

1871.

CONTENTS

PREFACE

A T a certain dinner, given by an Amphitryon who owned a faculty for collecting around him the most incongruous elements of social chemistry, an incident happened which I will take leave to note.

The wine had circulated; cigars were alight; and the usual (buttered) toast had been handed round. The hero of the evening had footstooled himself into the attitude of a troubadour, and had roared as gently as a sucking-dove to the twanging of a Spanish guitar. Somebody, "more Irish and less nice," had sustained the fainting revel by warbling *Eily Aroon*, and there was a rumour that a travelling journalist, who had condescended to visit Melbourne on his way to the Grand Pacific Slope, was about to temporarily abandon the abodes of sweetness and light, and sing "Whisky in the jar"—at which he was an adept. The comic gentleman had concluded his imitation of Mr. Charles Kean or Mr. Joseph Jefferson (I forget which one it was, but I thought at the time it was remarkably like one or other of them), and was dangerously near the abyss of his only song, when a tall brown person arose and gravely proposed the health of

"THE PIONEERS OF CIVILIZATION."

The idea was received with enthusiasm, and the brown gentleman went on to state how the Pioneers had driven their own bullocks, and washed their own shirts, and blacked their own boots, and kissed their own wives, and done everything, in fact, that the ordinary usage of our modern civilization demands to be done by somebody else. The brown gentleman was cheered to the echo ; indeed, when he described how, in a moment of agonised Pioneering, he had actually used his own tooth-brush, I thought the window-glass would have shattered. If he had told us how he had dug his own grave, we would not have been more delighted.

In considering upon the compliment paid me by Mr. Money, when he asked me to write a preface to this record of rough and ready bush-wandering, I think of the "Pioneer" of that dinner party, and, comparing him with other "Pioneers," find myself slightly ashamed of the noise I made at the hearing of his speech, and regret the four cut tumblers I broke by thumping on the table. Being informed afterwards that the Pioneer was, in the language of bush, "the best single-handed pitcher between Williamstown and Wagga," I have come to the conclusion that the outlay in glass-ware was an extravagance. But, to turn from the Pioneer of Fiction—who has done everything for himself but meet his bills—to the Pioneer of Fact, is a little difficult. By dint of "blowing," the pioneering bladder has swollen to the size of the paragraphic pumpkin. From a modest "plant," it has become an enormous tree whose roots stretch far underground, and beneath whose branches all sorts of jovial birds roost, feathering their nests the while. It is lamentable to witness the discomfiture of your after-dinner Colonist, when he meets with some unpretending fellow (who does not even swear), but who has "humped his swag" into strange lands, and traversed the "wallaby-track" under the direst conditions. The wind-bag, metaphorically "sat

upon," collapses with a long, low whistle, and another of the
illusions of our trusting new-chum-hood vanishes for ever.

Of young gentlemen who come to these colonies unpro-
vided with previously expatriated parents, the anxious eye
of the philosopher and the night cabman discerns two
classes—the young gentleman who "loafs," and the young
gentleman who works.

The career of the former hero can be predicted with
accuracy. Born of poor and absurdly honest parents, his
boyhood is passed in dreading the shop-counter to which
Fortune has doomed him. Family reasons (into which an
impatience of restraint and a fatal leaning to vulgar debauch-
eries largely enter) secure for the ingenious lad a passage in
the *Marco Polo* and a letter of credit for £100. His
mother weeps, his uncle smiles, and his little brother rises at
school to the dignity of a "fellow with a brother in Australia." Arrived at Melbourne, our hero astonishes Collins
street with the amplitude of his collars, and lounges the
Adonis of a Bourke street bar for at least a fortnight. He
drives a buggy, is going "up-country," becomes intoxicated
at noonday, hectors it at Cleal's, and discourses profoundly
on life in London from the gallery of the Oriental Café.
If his money only lasted, he would brilliantly anticipate his
natural end by a premature idiocy; but Fate and the Bank-
manager conjoining to prevent such a contingency, the crea-
ture sustains life on "forty pounds a-year and his tucker" at
the remote station of a transported friend of the family. Any
person with a taste for "curios" can purchase specimens of
this species for sixpence a dozen in Paddy's Market the day
after the *Great Britain* has anchored in Hobson's Bay.

The young gentleman who "works," however, is of a
diferent nature. It is not improbable that he is poor, but it
is quite certain that he is proud. He may have had a fortune once—and spent it, as young gentlemen will do—but

he does not whine about the inconveniences of a young colony, and, while anathematizing *Scott's*, prattle vaguely of *Very* and *Véfour's*. Being a gentleman, he does not look with contempt upon such of his fellow-creatures as are poorer in goods or education than himself. Being a gentleman also, though ashamed to beg, he does not disdain to follow the example of his ancestor Adam (of Eden), and dig as long as muscle and sinew cling together. This is the sort of young gentleman who "pioneers," who—with the most sublime unconsciousness that he is doing anything worth mentioning—travels across untrodden ways of bush and sand, swims rivers, scales mountains, lives upon the prey of his bow and his spear, camps affably with savages, "chums in" with diggers, and, in honest faith that to earn a "damper and a billy of tea" by hard work is better than to eat the bread of idleness at the expense of his friends, "knocks about" in the wilderness for three years, and appears one day amongst us flaccid-muscled pale-faces with a story "which he doesn't see much in," but which such folk as yet value unpretending records of kindliness and courage will read with interest.

Those who—freedmen of the rolling Australian plains —have slept uncanopied beneath the Southern Cross, have breathed the intoxicating perfume of the burning Australian noon, and know the subtle odours of the summer midnight— those who have learnt the strange charm of loneliness that dwells in the barren bush—will understand the fascination which a nomad life has had for the author of this narrative.

Those who—dwellers in cities—clothed in purple and fine linen, feed sumptuously every day, will have an opportunity to read a truthful account—picturesque in its very plainness —of the sort of difficulty which pioneering Englishmen make light of, by dint of luck, pluck, and good spirits.

MARCUS CLARKE.

KNOCKING ABOUT

IN NEW ZEALAND.

CHAPTER I.

THE afternoon of the 1st July, 1861, found me enjoying a white-bait dinner at Blackwall, being the last I should partake of on English ground for at least a considerable time. I bade, however, "dull care begone," and merrily pledged my dear father in a very decent brew of "cider-cup," trusting that we might be permitted to meet again after perhaps the lapse of years. I had no brilliant future before me, no pleasant little sinecure to look forward to in a new country, upon which to build up prospects of ease and "*dolce far niente;*" but a world to face for the first time, with no more powerful weapons than the love of adventure and a constitutionally sanguine temperament.

A passage paid, first-class, in an emigrant ship, and the smallest note the Bank of England issues in a corner of my waistcoat pocket, together with a hetero-

geneous collection of clothes, one of Key's cornets (a
present from my father, to enable me at least to make
a noise in the new world to which I was bound), and
a silver watch, were all my personal property as I
stepped on board the "Royal Stuart" at Gravesend.

After the usual bustle, caused by the parting of
friends, the lowering of boxes into the hold, and a
general disposal of people into their various berths, had
subsided, we found ourselves in the saloon a society of
twenty persons, the majority of whom were under
the rather juvenile age of twenty-five years. Half of the
entire cuddy berths were occupied by a wealthy Canterbury squatter, who, having been one of the first working-
men in the settlement, had taken such good care of the
pence that the pounds tumbled into his pocket. His
wife, sister-in-law, niece, children, and their nurse,
accompanied him, and formed a little court of which
the worthy man was autocrat. Three young fellows
and myself revelled in the luxury of a stern cabin,
with two fine windows, a bath room, and other con-
veniences. One of these, C——, was a clever, gentleman-
like fellow, who had entered Woolwich *en route* for the
service; but, having unfortunately acquired a *penchant*
for opium-eating, had found himself so shattered in
health as to render any hopes of a military career out
of the question. After recovering from the baneful
effects of the long-continued indulgence, he had determined to try the rough life of a colonist; and, as he
said himself, " knock the nonsense out of his system."
He had dined at my father's house a few days before

we sailed, and was liked by every one, so we at once formed a close intimacy, which I, for my part, shall feel proud to continue as long as we both shall live.

Feeling a dearth of excitement or amusement in our little world, we, that is to say C—— and I, organized a weekly journal, and placed at the door of the saloon an editor's box of formidable dimensions, with a huge slit in the lid for the insertion of any contributions offered either by passengers, emigrants or sailors. Among these we could boast of some talent that neither *Fraser* nor *Bentley* need have blushed to own on their staff of contributors. Narratives of Mont Blanc ascents with Albert Smith, from one of his fellow-travellers ; comical episodes of life and character, from a handsome pianoforte playing young Heidelbergian ; articles on the constitution and political history of New Zealand, from the pen of Mr. Hall, one of the leading states-men at the present moment in that country ; papers on duck and wild-fowl shooting, stalking, etc., by an " Old Shekarry ;" together with scraps of original and burlesque poetry, *on dits* of local interest, and a goodly array of jokes, conundrums, and answers to correspondents, stretched the modest little couple of sheets, to which we had at first confined our ambition, to eight well-filled pages of foolscap, published every Saturday afternoon in a leather binding. They were passed from the " cuddy " to the second class, thence to the " house on deck," then to the emigrants and sailors, and afterwards returned to the editor's office, in time for the removal of the old and insertion of the new paper. No personalities were permitted to appear, and the entire tone of the journal was essentially one of good-fellowship.

Finding this succeed after the first week better than we had anticipated, we started theatricals, concerts, and other amusements, twice a week; in which every one, from high to low, assisted more or less; and in this way our voyage was rendered at least partially free from the intense *ennui* which is the chief ingredient in a long trip where there is scarcely a change of scene from shore to shore. Such were our sources of occupation, and we became, moreover, considerable adepts in catching albatrosses, sea-gulls, whale-birds and molly-mauks, by means of long threads of cotton flying out astern in the breeze, in which these birds became entangled and were easily secured by an expert "angler."

Passing the Line was accompanied by the usual traditionary ceremonies, which now-a-days are familiar to every one; and after an agreeable passage of 97 days, we rounded the southern point of Nova Zealandia, anchoring a day or two after in Lyttelton Harbour, the port of the Canterbury Province.

Except that the hills in the back ground are not equal in height to those at the Antipodes, one or two of the small towns on the coast of Cornwall, surrounded on three sides by green ascents, would give a very good impression of the picturesque little town of Lyttelton. C—— and I were among the first who landed; and after visiting the post-office we struck straight across the country, and up the face of the steep hill behind the town. After reaching Christchurch, we walked back the same way ; being a distance of sixteen miles, over rough ground, which was not a contemptible tramp after three months on ship board.

There was not, on the whole, nearly so much difference as I expected to find between the manners and customs of New Zealand and those of the "old country."

The most entire civility was shewn to all strangers on arrival ; the welcome greeting given by tradesmen or others with whom we were brought in contact was perfectly sincere. People in general dined, drank, and dressed much the same as those we had left behind ; and on the night of our arrival, Farquhar, one of my fellow-passengers, invited some of us to a champagne supper, very similar to many a college "wine," and most creditably prepared by Julian, the worthy landlord of the "Mitre," which of course ended, like all jolly meetings of the kind, in furious fun and subsequent fog. We were all rather amused in the course of a day or two to hear of the niece of our worthy squatter before referred to being engaged as chamber-maid at an hotel in the town, that gentleman having turned her adrift to shift for herself. Being a plucky young lady, she, in colonial phraseology, "shaped" so well, that before a year was over she had married a gentleman holding a respectable position in the town, and has now been for some time a happy wife and mother.

At this time there were wonderful reports from the diggings, which had been discovered a month or so before we landed, and I should have gone there instanter, but that I was anxious to obtain letters with enclosures " of a pecuniary nature " from home. While awaiting their arrival, being somewhat stranded for want of means, I presented a letter of introduction with which I was provided to Mr. C. Wilson, a gentleman who resided a few miles from the town of Christchurch, and entered his service as cadet, a position which I soon found utterly foreign to my taste. This military designation of cadet was applied to any young fellow who was attached to a sheep or cattle station in the same capacity as myself. He was neither " flesh, nor fowl, nor good red herring," neither master nor man. In consideration of his " education," he was permitted to reside and take his meals with the master, but was sent to work with the men—the essential difference between the latter and himself being that they were paid for their labour, whilst he was considered sufficiently rewarded in having the " honour" to drink his "*pannikin*" of tea at the boss's deal table, where he was not half so comfortable, or half so much at his ease, as the men in their tent or hut. However, after a pleasant enough week at Cashmere, enjoying all the comforts of an English residence, we rode up to the station one fine morning, where we were to remain till shearing was over. A few words may suffice to give the reader a general idea of a station. There was the usual manager's house, with a loft for the accommodation of the hands who preferred it to the woolshed, where the sheep were shorn and the wool packed in bales for transmission home. There was the stockyard, a square enclosure with high posts and rails, into which the cattle, horses, &c., were driven when required for milking or other purposes; besides a hut or two for the shepherds about the run. There were the various out-houses, pigstyes, &c., that are the adjuncts of most dwellings of the better sort in the colonies. A mile or so distant was the pool where the sheep were washed, approached by yards (*i.e.*, passages and squares composed of hurdles or fences) leading to the dip, an enclosed floor, resting on a pivot, which, when filled with sheep tilted up, and shot the unsuspecting "jumbucks" into the water below.

In Mr. Wilson's neighbourhood were other large sheep farmers, and a public-house was being erected on the other side of a large and rapid river, flowing down over enormous boulders, a few hundred yards from the manager's house. The run itself was almost a perfect level, being on the Canterbury plains, but on the further side of the river Mount Peel rose some thousand feet, with wooded gullies breaking its smooth sides. A small kitchen-garden attached to the house afforded a few luxuries, such as young potatoes, carrots, and other vegetables, but no fruit of any description.

After a few weeks up here, the washing and shearing being ended, I bade an affectionate farewell to Mr. W—— and staff; and having in the meantime obtained the letters I had been expecting, with their very acceptable contents, I put an old railway rug on the top of one of the wool drays, and went down to Christchurch on my

way to the " diggings " in Otago, the southern province
of the island.

I took my passage at Port Lyttelton in the " Julia
Ann," a small craft of some thirty tons burden. We
were fifteen passengers in number, and, as the hold was
pretty well loaded with stores of all descriptions, and
not of the most odoriferous character, and as also two
large dogs were chained in it during the whole of the
trip, it is scarcely to be wondered at that, although
usually a first-rate sailor, I should have suffered somewhat on that occasion.

Before many hours, however, we were out of our
misery, and found ourselves drinking cocktails, con-
cocted by a flash barman, in a worked dress-shirt with
alarming studs, at the bar of the Provincial Hotel,
Dunedin, at that time the capital of the southern
settlement.

The town was filled with some thousands of men,
and the most lugubrious reports were in circulation.
By the accounts heard on all sides rheumatism, fever,
and ague were prevalent, the weather was frightfully
bad, and the country flooded. To go up the country
to dig for gold seemed to be merely going to dig one's
grave, while, in addition to all this, the scarcity of gold
was loudly asserted by most of those who had returned
from the diggings.

I had always a great idea of the wisdom of the
young lady who, when warned by her mother against
balls and other dissipations with the assurance that
both her father and herself had seen the folly of such

things long ago, replied naively that " she wished to see the folly of them too." So, in spite of all I heard, I started the second morning after my arrival, with my rug and blankets on my back (such a bundle being called a " swag "), and found myself in Gabriel's Gully in a day and a-half.

It was, as the favorite novelist of my boyhood might have remarked, towards the afternoon of a fine day in summer that two travellers might have been seen skirting the summit of a line of hills which overlooked a town that gleamed snow-white in the plain below. The town was surrounded by a vast net-work of holes of every shape and size, with heaps of variously colored gravel beside them, stretching away as far as the eye could reach, till they were hidden by the turn of the valley. This was Wetherstone's Gully, called after one of the first men who found gold in that locality, and who was, I believe, a shepherd—" Gully " meaning nothing more than a strip of ground lying between two hills, and having a "creek" flowing down its centre. One of the two travellers might have seen some three-and-twenty summers, for the down was scarcely yet visible on his cheek. This youth was no other than your humble servant.

Crossing Wetherstone's Gully at the highest ground, where the largest finds of gold had taken place, and which was called the Blue Spur, I followed the bend of the hills till I arrived in the centre of Gabriel's Gully. Here were canvas and galvanized iron stores, public-houses, restaurants, shanties of all descriptions and with every conceivable name, scattered around in all directions; while advertisements of nigger minstrels, gold buyers' prices, and placards, were flaunting everywhere. Leaving this, I made my way up the hill towards the police camp, where my fellow-passenger, Farquhar, whom I mentioned as having given a jolly supper on landing, and who had preceded me to the diggings, had put up an extensive stable, capable of holding some thirty horses ; he was as hospitable as ever, and after dining and spending the evening with him, I slept for the first time "on the diggings ;" and though by no means a Sybarite, I confess I would have preferred a warm bed after my tramp to the slab table with which I was compelled to content myself, every bunk and bed-place being preoccupied, and a couple of blankets and a corner of a bench being considered a lucky claim.   Farquhar had a manager to conduct the business of his stable, Ramsay by name, of good family like himself, and a terrible radical who had run through everything at home.   He was a man of herculean build and proportions, and was reputed, when staying on one occasion at Government House, Melbourne, to have thrashed the then champion of the Victoria P.R. The story ran that that worthy professional, when returning from the races, persisted in keeping his trap crawling at a slow pace exactly in front of the four-in-hand drag that Ramsay was driving, with the mistaken idea of taking a bit of a "rise" out of a swell ; in this he proved woefully at fault, for " the Corinthian," after having civilly requested the pugilist to go a-head or to one side, handed the ribands to a friend beside him, alighted on the road, and invited "the man of fives" to a speedy adjustment of their differences. Anyone looking at Ramsay would appreciate the force of the "reasoning" that acted so powerfully on the champion, who speedily "fell" to terms, and, the obstructing vehicle being removed, had leisure to admire the style of his antagonist, through his fast-closing eyes, as the triumphant car of the victor drove off at an Epsom pace to Melbourne.

Opposite to Farquhar's stable was a calico store, some 7 or 8 feet high, and about 10 by 12 feet in area; a few planks from old brandy and gin cases, nailed on saplings driven into the ground, formed the counter, on which were heaped the principal ingredients of a digger's domestic requirements—viz., sides of bacon, a tub or so of butter, one or two dry cheeses, sardines, lobsters, salmon, and other potted fishes and meats, bread, tobacco, clay pipes, and piled-up boxes of Letch-ford's vesta matches. The whole of this extensive warehouse was about as large as a reasonably-sized dog-kennel, and had an apartment behind, separated from the front shop by an almost transparent piece of calico. I was at Farquhar's door when my attention was attracted to the store by the natty appearance and manner of its proprietor. On questioning Farquhar about him, he offered to take me over and introduce me. "You'd hardly take him for a Harrow man from his surroundings," said Farquhar; "but he is so, and one of the best fellows going." In two minutes we had

shaken hands, and on entering the den behind the
"shop" I found a party of six or eight seated round
an old gin case, turned up to act as a table, and deep
in "unlimited loo," which, from the piles of gold and
sovereigns at the elbows of some of the party, and
their generally haggard appearance, must have lasted
for more hours than they could probably enumerate
just then.

Never having numbered gambling among my little
weaknesses, I did not join them, though made at once
a "brother of the order;" but, taking a seat on the
bunk, I mused on the strange vicissitudes that had
brought to this place and thrown together men of
such various positions in society. Here was a well-
trained moustache next to me, whose smooth and
wavy "fall" had been the envy of the wearer's subs
in the Lancers. Opposite was the son of a wealthy
wine-merchant, to whom his father was in the habit
of sending consignments of tawny port and golden
sherry, which enabled this worthy son to keep the
ball rolling, as he said, but never by any chance to
return to the old gentleman a percentage on his in-
vestments. Another Harrovian, for some years a clerk
in a Government office, one of the most high-principled
and perfect gentlemen I ever met, but with a bushel
or two of his wild oats yet unsown, was a third;
while a doctor, a trooper from the police camp (who
had commanded a troop of his own in days gone by),
with Farquhar and our host, made up the remainder of
the group.

In the afternoon of the day after my arrival I walked over to Wetherstone's, to hunt up the office of a gold buyer, whose brother, having been the college friend of one of my uncles, had written over about me. I soon found him, and he immediately asked me to stay with him for a few days while I looked about me. I accepted his offer, and for a week enjoyed myself exceedingly, meeting many whose histories would fill volumes with interesting matter and startling incident. Happening one day to catch a name that I remembered well, having been at my first school under a lady who bore it, and having known her sons well, both then and afterwards, I walked down with Fitzgerald from his office to the public-house whose proprietor bore the appellation so familiar to me, and there behind the bar of the "White Star" was Reinecker, not in the least altered, serving a "nobbler" to a sashed and booted digger.

CHAPTER II.

ABOUT a week after my arrival at the diggings,
Fitzgerald arranged a party for the Lammerlaw
Creek; so we made up our swags and took the road,
he leaving his business in charge of his partner.
We were a pleasant company; first, Fitzgerald himself,
a man of good old Irish family, tall, powerfully built,
and a splendid workman with either pick or sledge-
hammer. His eldest brother is described in the life of
Napier as having been the bravest and most powerful
officer in his army; while another is considered the
ablest writer and speaker on political questions of New
Zealand; the church, army, and navy being severally
adorned with the eloquence and gallantry of the
remaining brothers. Fitzgerald has since been himself
appointed to a very high position in the Canterbury
Province, which he fills to the satisfaction of all. The
second of our party was, and still is I believe, a Fellow
of Trinity College, Cambridge, and had been for some
years a tutor there; a most upright, good-hearted
fellow, who had since risen to a position of even higher
responsibility than his friend Fitzgerald. The third
was an Oxford Graduate, who, being a clever carpenter,
accompanied us chiefly in that capacity. A son of the
late Archdeacon of Akeroa, a fine young fellow,
only a year or so released from the Christchurch
Grammar School, with the writer of these recollections,
completed our number.

Under the superintendence of Fitzgerald, we worked
on the Creek for about three months, getting very fair
gold, though the great labour and expense necessitated
in fluming off the water consumed more time and money
than we could recover out of the claim. Every stick
of timber we required, and this was no small amount,
we carried over hill and vale, some three miles, and
paid one shilling a foot for every piece of sawn
material fresh from the pit.

It might be interesting to those who have not
happened to meet with details of this sort of life, to
describe the way in which our first piece of ground
was worked. The creek, when not swelled by heavy
rains, was some fifteen or twenty feet across, though
occasionally, as in our part, it narrowed considerably,
and ran through a little gorge of rock not above 7 or
8 feet in width. We had two waterfalls, one at each
end of the claim ; the one above being only 4 feet in
height, while the lower one, which fell out of our
ground into that of our neighbours' beyond, was nearly
15 feet.

Our object was to make a " flume," or aqueduct,
which should carry the water of the creek above our
heads, and allow us to work in the bed of it below.
We first made a dam across the creek with large sacks,
of which we bought 60 or 70 at two shillings each ;
filling them with soil, and sewing up the ends. These
we stamped well down, tier above tier, from bank to
bank, and strengthened with sods or squares of turf,
filling up every crevice. In this way we raised the

creek water, at the little fall above-mentioned, to the height of some ten feet.

Meanwhile, our Oxonian "chips" had prepared three boxes or sluices, open at both ends, each 12 feet in length, 2 in width, and 1 in depth, made of inch boards, riveted underneath, with small strips of wood nailed across. We now planted props or posts in the bed of the creek, upon which we fastened boards, taking care to have them so nearly on a level with the summit of the dam as merely to allow of a slight fall for the water in passing through the boxes. The boxes were then placed upon the supporting boards, the joins being stopped up with bullock hide. An opening being now cut in the dam of the same width as the mouth of the boxes, the water was forced into its new channel some 14 feet above our heads, till it arrived on the lower side of our ground. Here we had prepared a race or ditch to receive it and carry it away, till it fell over the rocks at the lower fall into our neighbours' ground below.

Then began the real business. Our cradle was set, our tools put in order, and we began to take up the ground in the bed of the creek to get down to the bottom, where the heaviest gold always lies in "pockets" or rock holes, and crevices. Having scarcely any water to bother us, and our dam holding very fairly, we got the best we could out of the claim in about six weeks, when, finding our next bit of ground not so good, we agreed to return to Wetherstone's and see if anything had turned up during our absence. Having "squared up," we struck the tents, packed our swags, and soon found ourselves again in the bustle of Wetherstone's busy street. Here the party broke up, Fitzgerald returning to his business, and the rest separating in different directions.

After a little while I found that billiards by day and "chimes at midnight" were not a bad prescription for relieving one's pocket of a tendency to plethora, so I went to work, and for the first time in my life earned a working man's wages. For three days I "did duty" on a puddling machine at the rate of 10s. a-day, until the "gaffer," finding me not equal to the others, who were all old hands, gave me the "sack." The owner of the machine, seeing that I was willing enough to work, and not over weak, gave me the billet of outside porter to a wholesale store belonging to him, of which I soon had almost entire charge.

About this time, though almost a "new chum" myself, I was much amused by a trio who arrived in the township and put up opposite my "shanty." . One of them was young Reid, my musical fellow passenger, whose talk was all of Bonn, Heidelberg, and student life in Vaterland, and who played the piano and sang remarkably well. He, like myself, had tried station work and had left it for the diggings, bringing up with him from Dunedin two young fellows just landed, twin sons of an artillery colonel, and just the lads to get on when the home rust was rubbed off them. Their costume first struck my attention. They had each a pair of leather shooting gaiters reaching to the thighs, velvet coats and waistcoats, and fur travelling

B

caps, and looked altogether very much like game-keepers. In a place where open shirts, moleskin trousers tucked into long boots, crimson sashes tied round the waist, and tall American wide-awakes, were the prevailing attire, it may be imagined that birds of such feathers were likely to be noticed, if not admired.

I gave them a hand in putting up a heavy canvas tent that they had bought on board the vessel in which they came out, and which they had been compelled to bring up on a dray. This having been done, and some bunks rigged, they laid in stores and prepared to "dig." I started them to cradle some "headings," or dirt thrown out of deserted holes, which had not been considered worth washing by the lucky boys who had originally sunk them and made their little "piles."

They knocked out in this day as much gold as sufficed to make them afterwards two rings, and then, for that time, gave it up. One of them walked down over the snowy ranges shortly afterwards with me to Dunedin, where he made a good living for some time by shooting ducks about the Taeri and selling the birds in the town.

In the meantime poor Reid, who did not care about pick and shovel work, was rather at a loss for employment, so on the first Sunday after their arrival I went round the township to see what was to be got. For some time nothing turned up that was at all suited to his talents until we found ourselves in a large room of the Ballarat Hotel, kept by an ex-*maitre d'armes* in the French service, who was the best fencer, I believe,

in the colonies. He had two most lovely children, and
many an hour I spent there in the evenings, enjoying
their innocent and affectionate ways, so great a contrast
to the scenes around. In the room there was a pianoforte, and before we had been there two minutes Reid
was hammering away at the " Marseillaise " with
tremendous energy. This gave me a cue, and I at once
spoke to De Lorée, and finding that his regular pianist
was absent at this time, and was doubtful of returning,
proposed Reid to him. After hearing Reid's best song,
" Who shall be fairest?" in which he rivalled Sims
Reeves, De Lorée offered him at once fifty shillings a
week and board and lodging, his duty being merely to
play for two hours every night except Sundays, the
rest of his time being at his own disposal. He accepted
this offer at once, and I got up a party the next night
to come and see him through his " first appearance."

The room was crammed with diggers of every
colour and nation, and though more than half of them
were in a state of conviviality, order was very fairly
kept. Now and then an excited Irish boy would try a
little roaring on his own account, and with much ges-
ticulation ask for a chorus. Reid's expression of face
on these occasions, or when summoned with a clap on
the back to " Give us ' The rattling boys,' lad," followed by a real Irish whoop, was a thing to remember.
The look which the beautiful *danseuse* bestowed on
the ruffian mob who forced her to execute one *pas seul*
before her execution could not have been more deeply
pathetic. The evening, however, passed off favourably,

and Reid soon became deservedly popular. I never saw him again, but I feel no doubt that his talents and *bonhommie* must always ensure him a friendly reception in any society into which he may be thrown. In the meantime I had started, on my own account, a circulating library, which paid me very fairly and returned a good percentage to my employer.

But I began to be gradually sensible of a constitutional longing for change, and wrote to Christchurch mail after mail for English letters, not wishing to leave while any chance remained of my receiving them. On one occasion I rode over to a " diggings " some miles off (Waitahuna), and by the merest chance happened to ask at the Post-office whether any letters were lying there for me. The answer was, " A bundle," which, it seems, had been accumulating there for some months.

After the receipt of these letters, I determined to delay no longer, but to make a start. I therefore set off with one of the amateur diggers before mentioned, and, after two days heavy tramp in the snow, arrived in Dunedin, from whence, after a sojourn of a day or two, I reached Christchurch in safety. Here I thought I deserved a spell, so I opened my boxes and assumed again the garb that is supposed to be indispensable to a gentleman in this 19th century. A month of good living and amusement soon gave me fresh desire for change, and I began to look about for an opening.

CHAPTER III.

*T*HERE was staying at the same hotel with me an old gentleman who had been one of the first settlers in the Province, and whose wife was called "The Mother of the Settlement." He often spoke to me of some quartz rocks that he had observed cropping out of the bush in parts of his station, which was situated in what was called the back country, *i. e.*, close to the ranges which divide the east from the west coast of the island. I at last determined to go up to those parts and have a look, for, as my readers may have heard, quartz is the mother of gold, and where-ever there is an abundance of it gold may reasonably be expected to exist somewhere in the neighbourhood. While I was endeavoring to form a plan for this purpose I unexpectedly met with an ally.

Rowland Davies, son of Archdeacon Davies, was at this time in Christchurch, and having been a digger in Australia, and a wanderer on the face of the earth, was very naturally as ready as myself to give the place a trial, more especially as Mr. Dampier, the squatter above-mentioned, spoke of the actual discovery of gold in the same neighbourhood by the former owner of the run. In addition to this recommendation as a mate, Rowley, as I afterwards called him, saved my life, or at least arrested a very painful and dangerous illness, by pre-scribing for me a strong remedy. Though he was then personally almost a stranger to me, he lay on the floor of my room for three nights watching me until I began to improve, and afterwards gradually brought me round.

Soon after my recovery we made our plans, and were much assisted by Mr. Dampier, who agreed to supply us with whatever meat, flour, or other necessaries we should require while prospecting.

All being arranged, I made up my swag again and started for Mr. Dampier's house, some twenty-five miles from Christchurch, at a place called Salt-water Creek. I was to remain here, by Mr. Dampier's invitation, for two or three days, until my new mate, who was at this time holding an appointment under the Canterbury Government, should complete his arrangements for resigning it, and should join me. My host was the representative of perhaps the oldest family in England, and could trace the line of his ancestors to Sir Guy de Dampier, who most indubitably did "come over with the Conqueror." He had a charming wife and daughter, and I spent three days there very pleasantly—the more so, as it would be the last taste of civilization that I should enjoy for some time, though I little thought then how long that time would be.

At this period servants of any description were not easily to be obtained, and I could not help comparing the readiness of the true lady to work cheerfully when it was required, with the squeamishness of those whom Thackeray would have brought under the head of "female snobs." I was strolling through the garden on the morning after my arrival, and came suddenly upon

Mrs. and Miss Dampier, with tucked-up skirts and bared arms. They were in an out-house, where, upon a slab table, Miss Dampier was peeling potatoes for dinner, and the old lady, as "jolly" as good health and good living could make her, washing clothes in a huge tub. Miss Dampier was a capital cook, and many a time, a few months after, did I look back to the cutlets and piquante sauce at her father's hospitable board, prepared by his daughter's fair hands.

At the end of the fourth day Rowley made his appearance, and after a last night in sheets and a good breakfast in the morning, we started, having some relics of Mr. Dampier's table for lunch, in the shape of spiced beef sandwiches, lined with Chutnee.

As our swags were a fair specimen of the usual burden which every man carries in the colonies when on the tramp to a diggings, or for a week's prospecting, I will briefly enumerate the contents of one of them. The blankets did duty as a carpet bag, holding pieces for patching, buttons, needles and thread, etc., tobacco, matches, and tucker, the latter comprising almost anything within the province of food. The roll of blankets was made as tight as could be, and tied with blades of the flax plant, so as to keep the contents from falling out ; a couple of strings, also made from flax blades, secured the swag to the shoulders of the bearer; a shovel was attached to each swag, and a pick, tin dish, and billy were also part of our load. With these we trudged away all the first day, on a metalled road, which got us a little into training, and, after two days' walking, arrived at the hut of a shepherd on Mr. Dampier's old station, where we stayed for a few days to sew our tent and make a few other preparations for prospecting the Virginia Valley, a few miles off. At the end of that time, with plenty of flour, soda, tartaric acid, and sugar in our swags, and some mutton, we scaled the hills and reached our scene of operations.

The valley was about a mile in width, and three in length, having formed the bed of an arm of the sea in the days when New Zealand was nothing more than a group of small islands; a creek flowed through the valley, winding over a small beach of shingle. The hut in which we were located had been the residence of the former manager of the run. It consisted at this time of only one small slab hut, with four bunks and a chimney; a couple of hundred yards away was an old wool shed, and also a small stable, both in ruins, while sundry turkeys, geese, and cats, that had been left behind, looked upon the neighbourhood as their home. The run had now been attached to a larger one bordering upon it, and together they formed the property of one of the largest sheep owners in the Province.

We stayed here some weeks sinking holes in the sides of the hills and in the river beds, but finding nothing richer than iron pyrites and rubies so small as to be of no value whatever. Quartz was plentiful enough, but none of it auriferous; and we were thinking of giving up the search in that locality, when we learnt from one of the shepherds that men had been sent by the Canterbury Government to prospect the valley, and the head of the Hurunui River, which ran through Mr. Dampier's station. Shortly afterwards, as we were returning home one afternoon, we met some of the party on their way to the tent. The boss was a fine fellow named Howitt, whom I afterwards knew well ; he was a relative of the well-known Australian traveller, who had volunteered in the expedition sent after Burke and Wills, those noble but unfortunate men who perished on their return after having been the first to successfully explore the great Australian continent. He and his party had also been unsuccessful, though they had travelled a long way up the Hurunui River, and had tried the ground that we had been prospecting (the Virginia Valley), and the rivers in the neighbourhood. He said that in a very few weeks the time that Government allowed him would have expired, and that then another party would be raised and placed at his disposal for the purpose of' making a good track up the east side of the dividing range, in order to see what sort of country there was to the westward. In that part of the island, even as late as 1864, there was not supposed to be a white man, according to a statement made by Mr. Long Wray, of Nelson, in a capital little pamphlet on New Zealand ; but this was not entirely correct, as will be seen.

Meantime, Rowley and I made up our minds to spend a week or two at the head of the South Hurunui, and there endeavour to push on over the saddle, and be the first to reach the West Coast.

I must here record one little episode of our visit to this solitary valley, where we had been, if not fortunate, at least comfortable and contented with our quiet life. One day, I had stayed at home while Rowley went out to work by himself, and I of course was to have a feed ready for him on his return in the evening. At this time we were nearly out of flour, and had been without meat for some days ; so I was sitting over the fire smoking and wondering what I could concoct out of such crude materials as flour and sugar, when the cackling of geese arrested my attention. These, as I before mentioned, had been left behind when the valley was deserted by the former owner of the run. We had frequently seen them about the out-houses, and in the bed of the creek, but, fearing they might be required by the new owner of the property, had hitherto abstained from disturbing the even tenor of their lives. At this moment, however, the sound of their cackling came upon my ears with an irresistibly attractive tone. Seizing my sheath-knife, I rushed from the hut. A few minutes of frenzied pursuit, a little flapping and shrieking, and I returned to the wharry with a magnificent goose under my arm. I slew him and plucked him in a trice ; and, cleansing out a big iron pot I found in the place, I popped him in. At this season (early in September), there were nearly all the vegetables we could wish for in the old gardens attached to the hut, even to sage and mint, etc., so that I had fair materials for a good cuisine. I filled the big pot with vegetables, packed neatly round my bird to within three inches of the top, and for seven long hours I kept the contents slowly simmering. I leave the reader to imagine what a dinner we made that evening, and how we even toasted one another in the soup *à la naturel*, better, as it seemed to us, than the richest turtle that ever graced the board of the Freemasons' Tavern. It requires a man to work hard and live poorly for a week or two to know the extacy of moments like these. I have marked the memory of that with a very white stone.

A few days after this aldermanic feast we were trudging along over the boulders of the Hurunui river bed, and in three or four days had our little tent pitched in the snow, less than half a mile from the glacier-covered ranges in which the river rises, and from the summit of which avalanches were constantly falling with a roar like artillery.

We were snug enough in our tiny home. Behind us half a sheep was suspended from the branch of a big tree, that had lain where it fell for many a year; the up-torn roots formed a fine break-wind, under the shelter of which we ensconced ourselves. Here we remained a fortnight, and, though for some days of that time we were unable to light a fire or stir out of the tent, being in fact almost snowed up, we managed during the few days of better weather to prospect most of the creeks in the neighbourhood, though with no success as regarded any discovery of "the colour." I am myself of opinion that the bed-rock on the eastern side of the dividing range is at so much greater a depth

than that on the west side, as to render it unlikely that
it would ever pay for the labour of sinking for a prospect, but time will shew.

We returned to the home station, where we stayed
a few days to recruit, and then made preparations for
joining Howitt, who had by this time started for the
Teremakau saddle with a fresh party from Christchurch.   Crossing the Hurunui River from Mr.
Dampier's home station, we ascended a low range, and,
passing Lake Mason, struck across a hill at the head of
it which overlooked Lake Sumner.   This was a lake of
considerable size, through which the waters of the
North Hurunui pass, entering at the upper end and
flowing out some miles below into a wild gorge, out of
which they descend into the plains of Canterbury.
At the foot of the hill, and just at the junction of the
Hurunui with the waters of the lake, we found a
diminutive wharry or grass hut, just big enough for
four persons to crawl into and pack close ; near this
was a " mi-mi," or shelter of a different description, to
be used as a safe repository for flour and other necessaries, besides paper or any articles that might attract
rats.   We recognised these at once as belonging to
Howitt, for there were bill-hooks with the government
mark on them, surveying materials, and other things,
in the recess ; so, though still early in the day, we made
up our beds in the little wharry for that night, that
we might make the 25 miles the next day with the
greater ease ; this would take us to the foot of the
saddle, where we expected to find Howitt.   With this

intention we were about to retire early, when we were surprised by a voice on the hills above us. We "coo'ed" instantly, and after a few minutes were joined by one of Howitt's party, with sixty pounds of flour. His arrival was of course a great help to us, as he had been up to the head of the North Hurunui, and knew the best fords and shortest cuts. The next evening, after crossing the river some twenty times, we reached the slab hut at the foot of the Teremakau saddle, so called from the river that ran down from it on the west side. Here we soon had a good fire and a billy of "skilligolee" to warm us up, while the bacon, dough-boys, and tea were being got under weigh. Howitt himself came over in the morning from the west side of the saddle, to meet his commissary and supplies, and to help in carrying it over to his party. He was not one of those paper-collar bushmen, who expect their men to do every thing while they look on, but always took his share of work or of tucker as one of themselves, and consequently gained more respect and esteem than would have been conceded to the strictest master, merely as such. He gave me my first lessons in bushcraft, such as a knowledge of edible herbs and roots, modes of crossing rivers, snaring birds, and many other invaluable "wrinkles."

After crossing the saddle we left Howitt and his party, and pushed on through the bush ; though unable to do more than a short distance each day, on account of the steepness of the forest-covered spurs over which we had to climb, forcing our way through the dense undergrowth which caught our swags at every step.

I can never forget the exciting moment when we first reached a point from which we could see the windings of the river Teremakau, which stole like the silver tresses of some ancient dame over its time-worn bed.

I do not think I am mistaken in believing that, with the exception of Mr. Leonard Harper, a son of the Right Rev. Bishop of Christchurch, who went over with a party of Maories some years before, Rowley and I were the first white men who reached Lake Brunner from the east side. A few Maories were in the habit of going over every year, by tracks only known to themselves, to see their friends at a pah or village on the Grey river, and with them Mr. Harper made his journey to the sea coast.

The river as we descended of course became wider and deeper, so that we were compelled to seek for fording places, which we had learnt by experience to choose at the bars or beaches above the falls, where the current was not so strong nor the water so deep as below the rapids, and the footing was therefore far better.

Rowley and I now agreed that, after reaching a good place for our first camp on the Teremakau, one of us should push on down the river, trying the creeks as he proceeded, while the other returned to the nearest station for more tucker, in the shape of flour, tea and sugar (meat, of course, was no longer to be thought of, though, thanks to Howitt's lessons, we could get ducks, crows, and wood-hens in abundance).

Acting on this agreement, we made one or two good

stages, and camped on a fine, open bit of shingle, out of reach of any but a very high flood. Here Rowley left me and started for the station, which it would take take him several days to reach, owing to the roughness of the track, the crossing and re-crossing of the rivers, and the density of the undergrowth through which he had to scramble, added to our ignorance of many shorter cuts and better tracks which we afterwards found out.

The first thing I did was to erect a little hut with bushes, etc. I then planted a stout sapling on a prominent part of the river bed, out of reach of floods, for a direction post, surrounding it with large boulder stones; on this I hoisted a red flag, torn from an old Crimean shirt, and also fastened to it a blade of the broad flax plant pointing towards to my rough little dwelling. These and other employments, such as baking my dampers, or "beggars on the coals," exploring the creeks that came tumbling down the wooded precipices on every side, snaring wood-hens, mending and washing my clothes, kept my time fully occupied; while an occasional dip into my only morsels of literature, a few numbers of *Household Words*, or a piece of the old newspaper I had brought in my swag, formed an agreeable intellectual excitement during the half-hour in which I smoked my evening pipe. This I did by the light of a good bush-fire, that danced and flickered on the trees and scrub around me, and showed the only living animals that formed my society—grey bush rats.

I will here describe the process by which Howitt had taught me to snare wild-fowl. The sport, as far as ducks were concerned, was simple enough. There was a species of grey duck with white bills, often described as the whistling duck. They were to be found at any time among the rocks, in creeks, or in the river itself, and, being very tame, were easily knocked over with a few stones, the only requisite being to keep below them, and throw up the stream.

For the capture of the wood-hen, however, very different measures were employed, in which considerable caution and patience were necessary. To describe the process à la Mrs. Glass: first cut two light sticks, one a few inches longer than the other; to the end of the shortest suspend, by a thin strip of the flax plant, a robin, or other small bird, newly killed; attach to the end of the longer stick a running noose, also of thin flax. When the game is first seen, take no apparent notice of its movements, but, holding the stick to which the robin is attached in the left hand, and the one with the noose in the right, dangle the robin a short distance from the ground, tossing it in the air to give it a semblance of life, and dropping it suddenly at times, as if in the agonies of death. This will sooner or later attract the attention of the wood-hen, and it will approach cunningly in order to seize its prey. Remain as motionless and unobservant as possible until it is within two or three feet of the bait, then slowly advance the right hand stick, and the moment the out-stretched neck of the wood-hen is seen through the noose, jerk the stick upwards, and the game is yours.

With crows a different plan again is used, one stick only being necessary; to its end attach a noose, not hanging down as for the wood-hen, but so fastened as to extend beyond the point of the stick, and in a line with it. The crow being very similar to our black bird, and seldom flying further than a few yards at a time, is generally found in low bushes, hopping from bough to bough. Noiselessly insinuating the snare between the leaves of the bush in which he is disporting, advance it gradually towards him, whistling or chirping at the same time, while he is occupied in listening, give the wrist a gentle turn, and all is over.

Nearly a fortnight passed, and as my mate shewed no signs of returning, I determined to follow him, even should I only obtain one pan of fried chops by the expedition. The weather was awful when I started, and I was anxious to get over the saddle and some way down the Hurunui as soon as possible, before a heavy "freshet" should descend and prevent my going either way.

On the evening of the second day I reached the old slab wharry that Howitt had built some way down on the east side of the saddle. I was surprised to see the smoke issuing out of the dilapidated chimney; but, concluding that it was Rowley on his return, I coo'ed loudly, and rushed in with a yell of welcome. I was received in a most warlike manner by two human beings, utterly unknown to me, whose astonishment was certainly equal to my own.

C

On the evening of a miserably wet day, in the heart
of a country generally considered the road to "nowhere," to come suddenly upon two strangers ensconced in an old hut was sufficiently startling ; but I
have thought since that *my* garb and air, with my
trousers tied round my neck, my hands full of bleeding
birds, an Adamite condition as to legs (which habit
I had acquired from Howitt, who travelled constantly
on bare poles), and the startling whoo-whoop ! with
which I leaped in at the door, like harlequin through
an advertisement of cheap clothing, was far more cal-
culated to upset their nerves.   They afterwards gravely
assured me that their imaginations depicted me as a
savage in his native wilds, with the blood of the cap-
tured birds, which he was in the habit of devouring
raw, crimsoning his hands, and with a possible inclina-
tion for the tenderest portion of the nearest human!

Mutual explanations, however, soon made us good
friends, and I shared their skilligolee—the best thing a
man can take in the bush when wet through and very
hungry—with hearty pleasure at having some one to
spin a yarn with again over the social pipe.   They had
set out, they told me, with the determination to reach,
if possible, the Buller River, which runs into the sea
on the west coast of the Nelson Province, a long way
north of the mouth of the Teremakau.

In vain I described the immense difficulties they
would have to surmount, even to reach the coast at all,
and explained the risks they would run of being delayed on the way, perhaps for weeks together, by the

rising of the river and its tributaries, to say nothing of the amount of "tucker" they would be compelled to carry with them, and the impossibility of returning if once they passed through the gorges of the river. They were in no way daunted by my accounts, but, on the contrary, were perfectly confident of success, and, like the world in general, would not heed advice, though given by one who spoke from hard-earned experience. They wished to "see the folly of it too," and bitterly, poor fellows, did they repent their determination.

I gave them all the hints I thought would be useful to them, especially about the snaring of wood-hens, which latter operation I demonstrated practically, and well was I afterwards repaid for the quarter of an hour thus occupied, for the recollection of it saved their lives.

On reaching the station, to visit which Rowley had left me, I learnt that he had sprained his foot on the road, and had gone over to Mr. Dampier's station, where our old friend the shepherd was nursing him most effectually, and that he had left a message for me, saying that he hoped to be right again in a very few days. Mr. Taylor, the gentleman to whom the station belonged, was a splendid fellow, and hospitality itself. He was most kind in pressing me to come up to his house, where his wife would do all she could to make me comfortable. I preferred, however, for more reasons than one, to await Rowley's return in the men's hut, and found McLeod (the shepherd) and the other hands first-rate companions. I became an immense chum with one of them, and he acquired from my descriptions such a passion for a wandering bush life, that he afterwards threw up his billet at Mr. Taylor's, and followed me all the way down to the coast, and round to the Buller River. He was an Oxford man, who, after taking his degree, had found himself too much in debt to hope to clear himself for some years, and was consequently now content with being a station-hand in New Zealand, on only £60 a year. Mr. Taylor told me that he was one of the best working men he had had on the place for some time, and an honest, generous, upright fellow into the bargain. Poor Charlie! His father, he told me, was vicar of some parish in the north of England, and that gentleman may possibly to this day be ignorant of the after fate of his son. He volunteered into the Colonial force in the Northern Island, and is supposed to have been either killed in action, or to have been one of three who were thrown from a dog-cart, and dashed to pieces over a precipice in the province of Auckland.

Good substantial mutton three times a day was to me a hearty enjoyment and a pleasant change of diet; and, by the time Rowley came over from Dampier's and joined me, I was in rattling trim for a tramp into the nethermost parts of the earth. Away we went with the full intention of getting a long way further down than we had yet been, before returning for any further supplies. We each carried a swag about eighty pounds in weight, consisting of the necessaries before alluded to, viz., flour, tea, sugar and tobacco. The afternoon of the fourth day found us in sight of the Red-flag Camp, as we had called the place where I had erected the little hut and direction-post.

On mounting the low, shrub-covered terrace on which I had pitched my camp above the reach of floods, what was our intense surprise to find the two men I had met in the hut. One was seated on the ground leaning against a small tree, his legs stretched out before him, gazing vacantly into space; his shirt was open to the waist, and every rib in his body was visible, while the space between his neck and collarbone was awfully distinct. The other was standing near him, supporting himself with one hand against a branch, while with the other he fluttered a piece of red rag at the end of a stick, evidently with the intention of attracting a wood-hen, but too far gone to recollect the absence of the noose, which, of course, was indispensable to its capture. Such a painful sight had never met my eyes, I think, before, as the quiet despair of the poor fellow on the ground, and the touching perseverance of the other in his vague endeavour to preserve life. They scarcely noticed us as we approached, though it was full a fortnight since I had met them on the saddle. We, of course, saw the state of things at a glance, and set to work to boil the billy as quickly as possible. In the meantime I got some cakes, which we had baked before starting, out of our swags, and placed one before each. I feel that the impression made by that scene has done more to make me alive to the sin of wastefulness than a thousand sermons. The gradual light that came into the eyes of both as their looks fell on the yellow pancakes, and the rush of awakened sensation with which they in frenzied haste seized and devoured them, was a lesson not to be forgotten by the most callous spectator. After slowly sipping a quantity of hot tea which we had prepared for them, and eating some more scone, they revived sufficiently to speak, though with great difficulty, both in so doing and in collecting their ideas.

Their account, as far as they could recollect, was simply this : they had been a considerable distance down the river, in fact, nearly as far as the farthest point to which I myself had pushed, and in crossing the river one of them had been carried off by the current, and his swag lost, containing, among other things, all that remained of their flour, matches and sugar. They had tried my plan of catching birds, but for some time had entirely failed in getting any ; and, finding none of the plants or roots I had described to them, they had, till the day before, actually existed for six days without food of any kind. On the morning of the previous day they had succeeded in snaring a woodhen, and had eaten it raw, but it only served as a whet to their raging appetite. Since the night before they remembered nothing at all.

We stayed a couple of hours with them, and, seeing that they were gradually coming round, gave them half our store of flour, and some tea and sugar, to enable them to reach Taylor's station without any difficulty ; and, being ourselves intensely desirous to get on, we did about a dozen miles further on our road that night.

We had turned into our blankets by the fire, and I was gazing at the Southern Cross above my head thinking of the sufferings of the poor fellows we had seen that day, when the thought struck me that they might possibly never reach even the saddle without assistance, and that in case anything further happened to them we should deeply regret it. I spoke of this to Rowley, hardly expecting he would be still awake, but he instantly agreed with me in resolving to return the next morning to assist them in at least getting over the saddle, and within a day's journey of Taylor's. This we accordingly did, and, finding that they had quitted the Red-flag Camp, we followed till we came up to them about half a mile on, evidently unable to proceed further. They had managed to keep an old single-barrelled gun with them throughout the journey, but as their powder and caps, we knew, had been rendered utterly useless by exposure to the wet, the first sight we obtained of these poor fellows proved to us that their faculties were still obscured. The sight was most touching ; one of them was kneeling with one knee on the stones, taking exact aim at a grey duck that was drying itself on a large boulder in the river. For full ten minutes he continued holding the piece and pulling the trigger down, cap after cap, till I went up and touched him on the shoulder. Rowley and I took his gun, and, carrying his swag, managed between us to lead them over the crossings ; and, after a long and disheartening trudge of some days, as it was the loss of precious moments to us, we reached Taylor's, where we left them to recover at leisure, and set off, post haste, on our way back. After this we got a long way down the river Teremakau, and established a permanent camp, close to a wide opening in the hills, which Rowley, after being absent a few days for the purpose of exploring, pronounced to be a large lake, surrounded with mountains and bush. This lake had been named some years before by the finder, Lake Brumer. My mate said he had been almost devoured by mosquitoes and sand-flies, and was very glad to get back into the old river-bed again.

It soon became necessary for one of us to return for more " tucker " and some tobacco, and again the lot fell on Rowley. So leaving me one morning with the rather dreary prospect before me of a ten days' solitude, he set off. A day or two after he had left I was surprised by a visit from three Maories, at a late hour in the evening, on their way to a native settlement at Kaipoi, a village about 20 miles from Christchurch. They did not prove very communicative, but, after an astonishing feed on wood-hens and fern root, they curled themselves up each in his blanket round the fire, and fell asleep. After watching the group thus formed for some time, I crawled into my " mi-mi," and was very soon asleep also. The Maories left me the next morning, and my time after this passed much in the same way as I have before described. A week wore away pleasantly enough, in spite of the curious sensation I experienced of being at so great a distance from any human being, and even the roughest form of civilization.

CHAPTER IV.

ANOTHER week passed, and no Rowley made his appearance. It had rained ceaselessly since he left, and the river had risen to a great height, when one night I was awakened by a roaring sound and a cold-bath sensation at the same time, which made me leap to my feet, and rush to the door of the tent, with a vague idea that the world had come to an end, and that I was merely perched on a corner of the chaotic mass, composed of half water, half land. It was as dark without as within. Not a foot could I penetrate into the pitchy blackness, and still louder and nearer came the thundering roar that had first started me out of the blankets.

I was camped on a high portion of the river-bed, where the scrub was pretty thick, and none but the very highest freshes could affect my safety; but the water, now reaching almost to my knees, shewed me plainly that the flood was increasing every moment; so, seizing a blanket out of the water in the tent, I ran for my life. I remembered, with a thrill of terror, that between the strip of higher ground on which I had been camped, and the bush range which was some fifty yards away, there was an old bed of one of the branches of the river, which would now be a torrent of fearful force and velocity. How I reached it, plunged in, and, half dead, contrived to crawl up the bank opposite, I scarcely know to this day. The rest of the night I was miserably cold. Drenched to the bone, and with one wet blanket in a dripping bush, I shivered till the morning. By that time the flood had gone down sufficiently to enable me to cross easily to where the tent still lay, attached to the pegs to which its sides had been made fast. One blanket caught in a branch, two or three soaking sticks of tobacco, a few pounds of flour, a shirt and cap held down by a shovel, and a tin dish, were about all the property the river had left me; but I was too thankful for my own escape to regret the loss of anything, however valuable. Another five minutes and my life's story would have ended in that howling, foaming river.

Taking this as a pretty strong warning, I moved the tent off the river bed, and pitched it upon the terrace where I had passed the night. The next day I began building a little "mi-mi," to serve as a resting place for the night in going back at any time for supplies; but finding that there were too many mosquitoes in the bush for any rest at night, I restored the tent to its former place, and commenced making a bridge across the old water-course, from the bank of the river bed, so that in case of another fresh coming down, I should be able to cross into the bush safely.

While I was working at this some days passed, and Rowley did not appear. Finding my little stock of flour had dwindled to a very few pounds, I baked it all into the form of small cakes, about the diameter of the top of a collar-box, allowing one a-day for ten days, and determined to trust to any birds I could procure for my chief subsistence. In this sport I soon acquired such dexterity that I had always a couple at least of wood-hens and ducks, or bush-crows, suspended from the ridge-pole of my tent.

My wharry and bridge finished, I became more than ever anxious for the arrival of my mate, as, my slender allowance of biscuit once gone, I should be compelled to start back, and might, if the river rose, and birds were scarce, have only the option left me to starve or to drown.

Three weeks had elapsed since Rowley left, and only three days' allowance remained of food. One night, when I was sitting deep in reverie, the gambols of the grey rats, as they came into the glare of the fire-logs, and chased each other even round my feet, attracted my attention, and it came into my head that there was no reason why they should not be good for food. No sooner did I conceive the thought than I acted upon it. I took a thick stick, and, in a watchful attitude, something like a trooper at " Attention," or preparing for " Cut one," waited motionless for the first that would come to meet its fate ; but, so knowing were they that, after trying for full two hours, I had only got two for my supper. These, however, after skinning and preparing, I cooked on spits of green wood, and most delicious morsels they were. This may perhaps be attributable to the fact of their feeding on roots, which are their sole support in the New Zealand bush, and I really believe they would be considered a delicacy at the table of the most refined epicure.

For two days I could get no birds with the exception of a wretched robin or two, and the fifth week had already begun with a continuous downfall of rain, which must, I knew, swell the river again in a very short time. My thoughts were occasionally pretty gloomy, and I pictured to myself my mate—for whom I had latterly felt a greater regard than ever, as I learnt to know and appreciate his unselfish and generous character—dashed to pieces at the bottom of one of the many hazardous precipices he must necessarily pass, or carried away down the relentless river, a death which has overtaken more victims in New Zealand than in any other spot on the face of the earth ; or, worse still, with a leg broken, or otherwise disabled, lying in some spot that I might never pass, calling in vain for help to the awful silence around, and with a horrible death from hunger and thirst awaiting his last hours. Many a poor fellow has left his bones to rot in the solitudes of the West Coast rivers and gullies since those days.

I never suffered these flights of fancy about Rowley to affect me to any extent, but directly they became too vivid I at once struck up " Cheer up, Sam," or "In the Strand," electrifying the more porks or "night-hawks" in the neighbourhood, till they flew to the tops of distant trees, and revenged themselves by repeating their mournful notes till I fell asleep. I had lived entirely on small birds for the last few days, and had kept my two remaining cakes as a last resource in case I should be compelled to start back. Late one evening I was busily engaged plucking a fine wood-hen, when I heard voices close to me. Dropping the bird in the fire, I ran towards the bush from whence the sound had seemed to come, and what was my satisfaction and delight to see a string of four men crossing my little bridge and coming down towards me. The first I recognised immediately as Howitt; the second, Rowley; and the others, two hands belonging to the Government party of which Howitt had charge.

Another hour saw the whole party under a temporary break-wind, with a roaring bush-fire hissing under the pouring rain, which tried in vain to extinguish it. Jack, the baker to Howitt's party, soon had cooking on hot stones thirty or forty large cakes that smelt sweeter to my nostrils than the most exquisite perfume; rashers of streaky English bacon were lying in a pan ready for frying; and the contents of a large billy were stewing on the cross-stick, from which the steam was indescribably appetising.

Rowley's leg had again caused him to delay his return, and, finding that Howitt had finished his track over the saddle, and was intending to advance further down the river, he waited a couple of days for him, and they had thus arrived together in the very nick of time. The yarns were longer and more interesting that night than under ordinary circumstances, and the hopes in which we indulged of finding both gold and fresh country were proportioned to our elation of spirits.

After a dinner which would have lasted me for three days a short time before, Howitt and I made an attempt to reach a point of bush from which we might

see somewhat of the run of the hills towards the lake
to which Rowley had already penetrated. Howitt,
with his usual dexterity, caught four wood-hens and
three crows during the time (only a few hours) that we
were absent. All we did that day was to trace the
direction by which Rowley had reached the side of the
lake. It lay through dense bush, standing in a vast
swamp, which accounted for the scarifying process he
had undergone from mosquitoes, etc.

The next day we went our different roads, Rowley
and I down the river, and Howitt to make his way
round to Lake Brunner, where he purposed to make a
stay of some weeks at least, and, in case of its proving
a good central point, to make it his head quarters, from
which thoroughly to explore the neighbourhood of the
lake. He gave us on leaving sixty pounds of flour, a
double-barelled gun, and a billy, which presents were
really almost worth their weight in gold to us then,
and we parted with mutual regret and good wishes.
We never saw Howitt again, poor fellow, for a few
months after, in the prime of youth, and strength, and
energy, he was drowned in crossing the very lake that
he had come so far to see and report upon.

After pursuing our way some miles further, the
river bed became wider, the river itself deeper, and the
gully on each side of us more precipitous. We came at
last to a stand still, not being able to cross further with
any degree of safety, on account of the depth and
rapidity of the current. So here we established a last
camp before going too far down to preclude the possi-

bility of a return, and then went back for the last time to procure a relay of tucker sufficient to last us down to the coast.

Our road being now familiar to us, we soon made our appearance at the old hut at Taylor's. A week of high living, novel reading, and sleeping, brought us up to Christmas day, and, being induced to stay a little longer, if only to recover from the effects consequent upon a large consumption of Scotch whisky, we had a final jollification on New Year's Day, and the next day, January 2, 1862, left with the expressed good wishes of all hands, and with the avowed intention of never again shewing our faces till we had accomplished our purpose of reaching the West Coast.

Whilst Rowley and I on our own behalf, and Howitt on that of the Government, had thus been working our way into the heart of a dense bush, with the hope of being the first to discover either a prospect of payable gold, or some open country fit for farming purposes, a few Maories had been finding a little fine gold about ten miles from the sea; and the news of this, as also of the fact that a Captain Dixon had landed at the mouth of the Teremakau and obtained gold, had excited the minds of the energetic Canterbury folks to such an extent, that parties had already left Christchurch and Kaiapoe to follow in our tracks, *en route* for the gold fields, which were already reported to be fabulously rich. Of this we knew nothing till the morning after we left Taylor's, when preparing for a start from the neighbourhood of Lake Sumner. I was tossing off

the last drop of coffee in my pannikin, when a man
with a horse suddenly appeared on the brow of the hill,
and was soon followed by more. They proved to be a
party from Kaiapoe, whither they had not long returned
from prospecting the Ashley, a river which, like the
Hurunui, runs down from the hills on the east side of
the range. Hearing the reports that were flying about
the country, they had made their way up with a pack-
horse, and were pleased to find we were going the same
way. We went with them as far as the saddle, but
then returned for some things we had left behind at
the hut on Lake Sumner, feeling sure that from our
knowledge of the country we could easily be among the
first to reach the scene of operations. As we were
once more preparing to travel we were joined by
another party from Kaiapoe, to whom Rowley and I
offered our services as guides, and we reached without
difficulty the camp we had last pitched, some miles
beyond the opening of the lake.

Here we began to find the river too unpleasantly
high and rapid for one man to cross. On one of our
party who attempted it being carried down and nearly
drowned, we adopted a plan constantly employed
by the Maories, and which Rowley and I had frequently found of great assistance. This was to form
line with either one good long sapling, or sticks and
guns, etc., joined together, held by the whole party
with both hands. By this means, keeping line exactly
up and down stream, the strongest and biggest of the
party at the top, and the others ranged in propor-

tion to their size, the difficulty becomes trifling; the
stalwart right-hand man has the whole brunt of the
swift current, while the others all bear up one against
the other towards him, and thus add their combined
strength to his; those toward the lower portion of the
line having little or no force of water to contend
against. All that is required is coolness and presence
of mind; if any one of the party becomes unnerved,
and so the line be broken, it is at once a case of "sauve
qui peut." In this manner, therefore, we contrived to
cross wherever it was necessary till we came to a river
that tumbled down a precipitous ravine, only a few
hundred feet from its junction with the Teremakau, into
which it fell. Here we were detained nearly a whole
day by one of the party refusing to venture into its
green waves, which rushed down over big boulders in a
decidedly evil-looking manner. We afterwards learnt
that the Maories had named this river "Typoo," which
means the devil, and there certainly was a spice of
devilry about its raging waters that suggested bad spirits
in a perpetual state of frenzied agony, struggling with
each other to reach the heaven of the broad and ma-
jestic river beyond. In another day the Teremakau
would be no longer fordable on foot. We stormed, we
abused, we entreated, but all to no purpose. Our ner-
vous mate was a comical little Irishman, with all the
fun and blarney of his nation, and not too much pluck.
Like the immortal Bob Acres, he was great things
when danger was past. By the camp-fire, over a
good feed and a pipe, he could draw upon a perfect *re-*

D

pertoire of good, though rather loose, and generally improbable yarns, in which he figured as the Munchausen
of the scenes he described. At last he agreed that if
half of us could cross easily, he would go over with
the rest ; so, although three was not nearly so safe a
number for crossing as the whole seven would have
been, Rowley, I, and one other, were obliged to risk our
lives to satisfy the obstinate Paddy, who was afterwards brought over, placed in the middle of the rest
of the party, clinging to the pole with all his might,
and with such an expression of misery on his pale
little phiz, that we could not help shouting with
laughter as he came across, looking neither to the
right nor the left, and evidently under the impression
that his last hour was at hand. That evening he
came out bolder than ever, and his comicalities and
broad fun soon made us forget the trouble he had
given.

The evening of the second day after this we arrived
at an immense flax swamp, where the river widened
out considerably before entering a narrow gorge, which
apparently continued unbroken for many miles, possibly even down to the sea coast.

Those who have seen the specimen of the New Zealand flax plant that was sent to the Paris Exhibition,
each with its spear-shaped leaves and brilliant blossoms,
will be able to picture to themselves the fine floral
display surrounding us.

The next morning we held a council of war. We
had packed our swags and attempted to cross the river,

but found it far too deep, so we sat ourselves down
upon the shingle, seriously to discuss the next step
that was to be taken. We could not go back, for to
say nothing of the chances of the river rising, which
it might do at any time, we had not sufficient supplies
to last us till we could reach the nearest station on the
east side. Our great object, therefore, was to get down
to the coast as soon as possible, and to reach some spot
where we could find Maories; till then we ran a fearful risk, as we had only two alternatives, either to
make some sort of raft which would carry us and our
swags, tools, &c., and float us down the river through
the gorges that loomed before us, or to take to the bush,
and, by forcing our way through brake and briar, over
precipices and torrents, reach the coast overland. To
this latter course I was strongly opposed, and was supported by the majority, for it seemed probable, from the
experience of more than one amongst us, that we
should meet with insurmountable difficulties in the
attempt. The sequel proved that I was right. Two
of the party, one of whom I forgot to mention as one
of those we found starving at the Red-flag Camp, were
undaunted enough to wish to brave the chances of the
bush again, and were bent on trying the overland route.
Seeing that they were determined, and remembering of
how little effect my advice had been on a former occasion, we let them go with a parting shout from me
to be sure and come back before two days were over
if they came back at all, as by that time all hands
would be aboard and ready for the voyage. Mean-

time we turned to at once to adopt the former plan, and, while old Bob Fergusson, who was a baker by trade, started his cooking arrangements, we began to collect dry flax-sticks out of the swamp, breaking them off close to the butt, and carrying them in bundles to the bank of the river, where the *mogueys** or rafts were to be launched when completed.

First of all, the sticks were laid side by side on the ground, the butts towards the centre, and the light and feathery tops towards each end. These were tied with blades of green flax, scorched in the fire to dry the slimy gum contained in them, and also to make them more tough and lasting. When the bottom had been fastened together in this manner, bundles similarly disposed were laid on the sides and lashed to the frame below, and the hollow thus formed was filled up with loose and broken flax-sticks, then another set of bundles were placed above the former ones, and filled in as before. Three layers having been lashed tightly down to the frame-work beneath, and also to each other, and the ends tied together in a point at the bow and stern, the moguey was complete. The first we made stood from three to four feet in height, according to the comparative ripeness of the flax-sticks, and capable of supporting two or three men and their swags with safety. When it is considered that these sticks are as light or even lighter than cork, it will readily be understood how well they would answer the purpose to which we applied them. We had no idea

* Maori name for a raupo or flax-stick raft.

how the Maories were in the habit of making their "mogueys," but we found ours subsequently to be very similar to theirs, and quite as serviceable.

On the morning of the next day, just as we were commencing the second raft, the two deserters hove in sight, having utterly failed in making any way in the bush, and consequently having returned in post haste to join us in time to start by water. Two days and a half sufficed to complete the mogueys, and the next morning we launched them, Rowley and I going aboard the first, three others managing the second, and Johnson and his mate on the third. Johnson's mate was a German, with a perfectly natural horror of cold water, and as soon as we started he laid himself flat on his stomach and clasped the sides of the moguey with both hands. In this order we launched our little fleet, and by punting with long sticks soon got into the current. Once fairly under weigh, steering was of no further use. We went down the rapid river like straws. For the first two miles it was jolly enough, and we were congratulating ourselves on the success and safety that had attended our venture, when, after rounding a long curve in the course of the river, we arrived in sight of a gorge into which the wide river narrowed, and rushed as through a millrace with foaming, seething violence. Our raft being ahead, we were the first to perceive the breakers as they dashed up against the rocks at the foot of the cliffs on the further side from us. We shouted a proposal to the others to try and get out of the stream and land at a

spot where we could see more of the place; but we
might as well have tried to stop a woman's tongue as
to stop our rafts. On we went, and nearer came the
danger : already we began to rock in the waves caused
by the drawing in of the funnel or gorge, and for full
two minutes I gave up all hope. Right in the face of
the main body of the water where it entered the gorge
was a mass of rocks, jumbled one upon another, at the
foot of a towering cliff, that frowned grimly down on
our adventurous little vessels as they approached
nearer and nearer. Splashed with spray on all sides,
tossed and tumbled by the various currents as they
met together, we drove on, helpless as infants, towards
the coming peril. I uttered a prayer not loud but
deep, and, clutching the fragile twigs beneath me,
awaited the fate that seemed inevitable.

Scarcely could I credit the evidence of my senses as
I felt myself flying, not against, but *past* the terrible
spot, and still more when we found our little moguey
suddenly floating safely in the centre of a lake-like ex-
panse of water, with the most beautifully-varied foliage
crowding the slopes of the ranges on each side of us.
The whole of that afternoon, with its dash of hazardous
adventure to give it a zest, often comes back to me
in day-dreams, like the sound of some sweet voice
heard above a chorus of discordant singers. A bright
sun gleaming far down the windings of the gorge, the
brilliant vermilion of rata blossoms relieving the varied
green and yellow of the forest trees high above us, and
our little bark floating peacefully on, except when now

and then it shot down a fall only to reach another waveless surface beyond.

I could not help laughing heartily, though I confess to have been alarmed enough myself, when, on looking back as soon as we had got out of reach of those unpleasant rocks, I caught sight of the fat German, his square face rigid with horror, and nothing of his person visible (so closely was he embracing the moguey) but his hands, which were convulsively clutching its side as he came on to what he must have conceived his doom. My feelings were shared by the little Irishman, who, having now some one to crow over, improved the occasion, and, perhaps with a view to smother the qualms which he must have experienced at such a moment, shouted and yelled vociferously. By the evening we were within a few miles of the sea, and reached a creek where the river became very broad, and consequently less rapid, so that we could easily beach our mogueys. Here we found the former party* whom we had guided as far as the saddle of the Teremakau. They were engaged with the Maories who had before found gold near the coast in sluicing some ground at the mouth of the creek. They were astonished beyond measure to see us, for they, it seemed, had had Maories with them who had put them up to their method of building mogueys, and who never imagined that any white men could find it out for themselves. We immediately made boxes and set to work to sluice some of the same terrace, but after

* These were Smart, Day, and party, from Kaiapoe.

trying for about a fortnight could get no gold to pay us. Rowley then started off for a few days' prospecting, but came back unsuccessful, bringing with him a nice piece of greenstone which he had picked up in the ranges at the head of the creek.

CHAPTER V.

E all had a very narrow escape at this time from the same fate that had before so nearly overtaken me. Our tents (three of them) were pitched in a row about fifty yards from the river, on pretty high ground, though still on the shingles. The creek that we had been working ran down on one side of us, and a smaller one on the other. One night, after hard rain for two or three days, I was awakened by my mate, whom I found shouting in my ear, while he hauled the blanket off me, " Be quick, Money, or you'll be too late! The river's up again!" I jumped up as quick as lightning, and, bundling what I could under my arm, ran inland. We all got safely across into the bush, but the next morning, on looking round at the water running several feet in depth over the spot where our tent had stood a few hours before, we gazed in each other's faces and expressed our thankfulness at the escape we had had. We lost several things in this flood, and, being utterly tired of the place, and short of "tucker" besides, Rowley and I determined to sell our gun, which was of scarcely any use to us, and reach if possible the Buller River by the sea coast. Two of the other party agreed to join us, and with a couple of Maories we started in a body for the Grey river, where there was a Maori village. This was the first occasion upon which I had ever heard the " tangi," or melancholy wailing, which is performed by

the women of a tribe on the departure and return, as
well as on the death, of one of its members. We were
accompanied by a Maori named Peter, who was returning from Kaiapoe after an absence of more than twenty
years, and the scene was therefore in celebration of the
event. They had, I suppose, been informed of his
approach by some of the boys who had come out to
meet us, and while we were still some way off we
heard the long, low, wailing notes of the "tangi,"
rising and falling like the vibrations of an Æolian harp.
When we came within view the women of the tribe
advanced with their heads bowed low to the ground,
and, covered with mats and shawls, kept up a
mournful moaning, now and then rocking themselves from side to side. After coming towards us a
short distance, they halted in a line, and as Peter
reached each in turn they rubbed noses with him, the
tears streaming down their faces while they still continued their lamentation. After this they all withdrew
to a wharry, and sat down on the ground around the
sides of the hut. For more than an hour the chief
people of the village came in and out with great
solemnity in their manner, and a general rubbing of
noses was carried on all round. We remained with
these good people three days, and were treated with as
much hospitality as any civilized people could have
shewn towards a few ragged, hungry adventurers like
ourselves. The old chief in particular was profuse in
his generosity. He went into the bush to obtain honey
for us ; he made his women prepare huge masses of

potatoes and salt "ka-ka" (the New Zealand parrot), and when we left, after buying thirty pounds of flour from him, he went out in the morning in his canoe and brought in a gigantic basket full of eels (over two hundred), which he gave to us "omi-nomi." It was a most astonishing haul, though of course nothing to any one accustomed to this kind of sport on old Father Thames at Teddington weir. We could not carry more than a few away with us, but we made some return for the kindness of the old chief by helping him to split open the rest, and to hang them on the fences of the village to dry in the sun ; when dry, they were almost as good eating as the celebrated Finnan haddock.

The three days' good living and rest at the "pah" completely set us up, especially as we had beautiful weather all the time. The first night after leaving the kind-hearted Maories of the *Mawhera*, we camped (or rather rested, for we did not pitch our ragged old tent) in a most charming spot. This was a natural cavity in the face of the cliff, with a ledge just wide enough for us all to lie down upon. Below us, as we sat sipping our pannikin of tea (which we had been compelled to boil at some distance and bring up to our den), were piles of rocks jutting into the sea, over which the waves came surging and roaring with "fine frenzy" almost to our feet, whilst out in the breakers, about a hundred yards away, was a weird-looking, weather-beaten rock, which Ocean in his most furious moods had lashed with unavailing fury for many a lustre, still, like some aged Christian standing firm

amidst the storms and violence of relentless persecu-
tion. It stood there giving rest to many a tired sea-
bird, or a home where it could rear its hardy offspring
in unapproachable security. The cave was so situated
as to shut out to those within it the view of the coast
on either side and the rocky points round which we
had been toiling all day; and I felt as if we were on
the bosom of a "world of waters," and our little plat-
form might be an island, round which might appear at
any moment, with their attendant dolphins and sea
monsters, Tritons and sea-nymphs from their coral
palaces far down in the cool green depths around us.
The sunset was wonderfully grand, and I indulged in
half-an-hour of that pleasing melancholy, so soft, so
impressive, and so impossible to analyse or explain,
which steals over one at the sound of remembered
music, or the sight of any solemn scene in nature that
seems to recall forgotten and undefinable bliss experienced in some previous state of existence long, long ago.

Rowley had seen far more of life than myself, and
knew its stern realities; the world no longer appeared
to him as it had hitherto done to me—a pleasant place
made for purposes of enjoyment only—and the experience thus gained had strengthened a naturally imagina-
tive and poetical mind, by engrafting on it a definite
apprehension of the real, without in the slightest degree
lessening his full appreciation of and admiration for the
ideal. A more valuable companion I could not well
have found, and as you could scarcely mention the
name of a work, from Boccaccio or Froissart's "Chro-

nicles" to "Verdant Green," that he was not acquainted with, we were seldom at a loss for agreeable conversations or discussions. Doubly in his society did I enjoy scenes like that I have just described.

On leaving this romantic spot, which we did next day, we proceeded on our way, crawling and climbing over the slimy rocks, sometimes leaping from one to the other over a raging cauldron of foaming waters that threw up their spray in clouds over our heads, making their stony surfaces as slippery as polished marble. This latter feat was very hard work when repeated all day long, with a swag weighing 60lbs. strapped to our shoulders. The flour that our two other mates had brought had been quickly consumed, and as we, of course, shared ours with them, and continued to do so as long as there was a grain in the bag, it soon began to exhibit symptoms of growing "beautifully less."

On the eighth day of our journey, in crossing a deep stream, our stock of matches was utterly ruined, and we were therefore compelled to eat our flour raw and to drink water instead of tea. Rowley and I, having had to do this more than once before, did not suffer from the privation; but one of our companions did so most acutely from his first meal of dough, and vowed he would sooner starve than touch it again. We found a good quantity of a bush plant called "nikou," the pith of which is much like hazel nut, and is very good eating when roasted or boiled. This and fern-root made a variety that enabled us to get on well enough for a day or two; but we were beginning to feel

queer on this diet, when one day we reached a number
of rocks covered with shell-fish of all sizes. Here was
a grand field for our sharpened appetites, and billy-full
after billy-full did we consume of the raw fish with
great gusto. We took a supply with us when we left
this place of plenty, and it was not till they were all
devoured, which, alas! was but a short time, that we
again felt the old gnawing sensation that dough would
not allay. I had a burning-glass among the odds and
ends of my ditty-bag, but the weather for the last few
days had been very bad, and without the sun no use
could be made of it.

On the eleventh day after our departure from the
Maories the sky cleared and out came the sun, and
never, I believe, were his rays more welcomed than by
us that afternoon. A short time before we had managed for the first time to knock over a red-bill and its
two young ones, and with the spunk from the bark of
a red pine and some of the lining of our pockets we
soon raised a flame, and such a picking of bones ensued
when the billy was taken off the fire as would have
done credit to a quartette of ravenous jackals.

This feed set us on our legs again, and for the next
forty-eight hours we got well on our way. About two
days' small rations of flour remained in our bag, when
we camped one afternoon on the edge of a perpendicular
cliff that stopped our further progress. No flax growing near by which to lower ourselves down, we made
a halt, and while one of the party cleared a place for
sleeping, and cut "feathers" or small branches of ferns

with his tomahawk for us to lie on, the rest cut their
way through the bush in hopes of reaching higher
ground, where we could see what sort of coast lay
beyond us. If we could but descend to the other side of
the wall of rock which at present barred our way, we hoped
still to be able to travel along the rocky points as before,
and at all events we could not lose our way so long as
we followed the bend of the coast. With this end in
view we worked hard till past sundown, and succeeded
in reaching more open bush before we returned to our
camp below. This we traversed the next morning, and,
finding plenty of robins, had a good dinner of robin
soup, with the robins themselves for second course. In
the afternoon we suddenly came out of the bush upon
an open pakihi* some miles in length, covered with
short fern and rushes. On the other side of this we
found a tree growing at the edge of a deep, thickly-
wooded ravine, upon which a Maori name was carved,
and close to it a sort of path which led us through the
bush and across the windings of a stream. It had
probably been made by Rochfort in one of his coast
surveys, and brought us out at last to the sea-coast
once more. That evening we all felt, I remember, very
low-spirited, not knowing how long it would take us
to reach the Buller, as we had already been a fortnight
on our way, and could as yet see no signs of neighbouring civilization. How true is it that when things
seem most gloomy to our eyes the brightness is nearest.

* From what I can ascertain, this spot must be the site of the
present town of Charleston.

All the next day we plodded drearily on, and the evening saw the last of our flour made into cakes and eaten. Our tea and sugar had long since been expended. Darker than ever seemed the prospect; neither fern nor " tucker " had met our eyes for some time, and the sands were unbroken by a single crag that could shelter a periwinkle, but not until the afternoon of the sixteenth day after leaving the " Grey" did we begin to straggle. Rowley went on ahead, I came next, and the other two followed at intervals, both of them suffering much from the state of their feet, one of them being entirely without boots, and the other quite unable to bear the pressure of them. That night we curled up dismally enough in our blankets, supperless and nearly hopeless, and slept deep and long till the glare of the sun and the furious bites of the sand-flies awoke us. Little did we dream, as we packed our swags with a sigh and a melancholy laugh at our condition, where we should lay our heads that night.

Bravely through that long hot day—for it was the hottest month of the New Zealand year—did our two companions bear up, though once or twice they well nigh succumbed in despair. I of course suffered somewhat, as I knew Rowley did also, but as we had the advantage of the several months' training in hard living and hard tramping, we naturally found the privation and endurance less trying than did our mates.

The close of the afternoon of the seventeenth day after our departure from the Maories with their comfortable wharries and luxurious abundance, found us trudging wearily along the sands of a long unbroken reach of coast line. About four miles back we had passed a point of rock which bore a strong resemblance to those which we had been led to expect, by the maps drawn on the sands at the "Grey" by the old chief for our guidance, we should meet with some ten miles from the Buller River. We had also seen, on the flat beach above us, signs of bush civilization consisting of an old saw-pit in the sand, with a rotten log still lying across it ready for sawing. My mate Rowley was a long way in advance of me, stepping out pluckily, and carrying the remains of his boots in one hand while the indispensable old billy occupied the other. My eyes had been fixed dreamily upon him for some time, as I mechanically plodded on, following the prints of his toes in the sand, while the other two followed a few hundred yards behind, when suddenly my half-closed eyes opened with astonishment to see his figure, which was lit up by the red sun as it declined in the waves, leaping and twisting itself into all kinds of wild contortions, and with no apparent reason for such a display at such a moment. At the same time the boots which he carried went flying into the air one after the other, followed by his ragged old Glengarry. After another series of demoniacal capers, accompanied with frantic cries, he threw his swag over his head, and on its coming to the ground danced upon it with pantomimic gestures indicative of sudden though confirmed lunacy. Feeling sure there could be but one cause for such a mad display, I hastened on

E

with a beating heart, and on arriving at Rowley's side became seized with a mania somewhat similar, and, as if bitten by a tarantula, went through an original sword-dance, minus the swords, till I was tired, ending the performance with the same finale as my mate.

There in full view, not above a mile from us round the bend of the bush, was the funnel and rigging of a steamer, lying in what we knew at a glance must be the Buller. Beyond, on the higher ground, were two or three huts and a wooden house, while indistinct forms moved to and fro in front of them. Our suspense was over ; already our mouths watered at the thought of the supper that we already pictured as awaiting us.

Jem and his mate soon joined us, and, though less demonstrative, were even more relieved and delighted at the sight than we had been. When we arrived on the beach opposite the little township and the steamer, we found the tide so high that, though eager enough to get across, even if we should have to swim for it, the distance was too great to be accomplished with our swags ; joining, therefore, our voices together, we gave vent to coo'ee after coo'ee, which went pealing over the water and let the inhabitants understand that we were anxious to cross over as soon as possible. After a slight stir among the group which collected on the beach, we saw a man get into a little boat from the steamer, and begin pulling across to us. We cheered him as he approached, and he was not long in reaching the extreme point where we had stationed ourselves. " Well, boys, where in all creation can you have sprung from ?" was our greeting from the bluff, thick-set, but withal good-hearted rough who had come to act as our Charon, and ferry us over to a land of plenty, or at least one of flour and potatoes and good salt horse. This fellow's astonishment was scarcely to be wondered at, for with the exception of the crews of one or two vessels that had been wrecked on the coast to the southward, and an expedition of Rochfort, the surveyor, returning from the " Grey," no white man had ever come from that direction, always excepting Mr. Leonard Harper, whom I mentioned as having crossed with a party of Maories some years before.

Our friend of the boat was at that time the proprietor of a small store, with rough, split, slab sides, and thatched roof, in which he was doing a good business, and was the most popular storekeeper in the township. He has since that time become one of the wealthiest wholesale merchants in the Grey district, with a township named after him, Blaketown. As he was the first to welcome us to the Buller, and to start us subsequently to the nearest diggings, from the day of my arrival I almost invariably obtained my stores from his place. I am not afraid that he will object to the mention of his name by " old Money. " May he continue to prosper. The amount of food we that night consumed was a severe drain on the hospitality of Mr. Waite, the leading storekeeper, who spread his table twice over before our voracity declared itself appeased.

The next day Rowley and I took a job from Blake

at the rate of 10s. each per day. This was to make
mortar, and with it to plaster the slabs that formed
the sides of the store, and also to assist him in carrying out other slabs ready split. A few days finished
this work, and enabled us to procure stores to take with
us up the Waimangaroa, a river we had determined to
try. This place had been a short time before the best
diggings in the neighbourhood, but a new rush having
broken out on the Lyell Creek, some distance up the
Buller itself, it was now deserted, save by some half
dozen miners who thought it a good chance to stick to
the old friend, while the multitude rushed to pay court
to the new. Accordingly, on Sunday afternoon we
laid in our stock, and as it was our last day in the
township we determined to get some dried apples, make
a good duff, and put on a pot of spuds, to partake of
which we invited our two travelling mates who had
shared our privations on the way from the Grey river.
The duff was made, the potatoes were boiled, a fine
piece of bacon was quietly simmering in the pot, with
plenty of sow thistles or Maori cabbage to give it a
flavour; and having hung up the billy of potatoes and
the duff to the ridge pole of the tent, to keep it from
the rats, we took a stroll before dinner. Our feelings
may be more easily imagined than described, when, on
our return, we found the open flour bag rolled in the
dust, full of holes, and the remains of the duff, bacon
and potatoes scattered in all directions by a small
colony of enterprising pigs, who, thinking by the smell
that titivated their inquisitive snouts so temptingly,

that the various luxuries around would by no means
disagree with them, had attacked everything indiscri-
minately, and left scarcely a "wrack behind!"

The Waimangaroa is a small river about ten miles to
the north of the Buller, and though the ground had
proved in general very "patchy," yet a large amount
of gold had been taken out, considering the small
number of hands that had been at work upon it.
Here we spent a month, merely making enough to pay
for a further supply of "tucker," and a few pounds
besides. Just at this time we heard from a stray prospector that the Nelson Government were about to
have a road made through the bush on the south side
of the Buller River up to the Lyell Creek and the other
diggings, and that Mr. Skete, the government surveyor, was taking on hands for that purpose. We all
determined to go down to the township, and get on
"the strength" of the company, as the wages were
very fair. Rowley and I applied the evening we
reached the Buller, and, finding that Mr. Skete
wanted a couple of hands for his canoe, we offered ourselves and were accepted. The coxswain was a good
sort of man, with a euphonious appellation, "Cincinnati
Bill," and for a month we got on famously. We received 10s. per day, "wet or dry," *i. e.*, whether we
were working or not, and provisions at Government
prices. The work was pretty hard sometimes, when a
heavy loading of stores had to be taken up the river;
for when we arrived at a fall or rapid, we two got out
of the canoe, leaving "Bill" to steer it with a pole, and

taking the end of a trail rope, 70 or 80 feet in length, over our shoulders, we did the work of barge-horses along a canal bank, with the slight variation in the duties of those animals that a swift current was rushing against us up to our hips at the rate of twelve "knots" an hour. Wet through, both day and night, in bad weather the only way we managed to keep ourselves moderately warm was by keeping up a flow of "spirits" within! The amount of Hollands or "square" which we consumed on these trips would have astonished one of the Viking race, and this too with no very visible effect either on our brains or constitution. We soon, however, wished for a change of employment, so we took a contract from Mr. Skete to clear a road twelve feet wide across a "Parkihi" or open piece of country, chiefly covered with fern and tea-tree (manuka) scrub, for a distance of three miles. For this, when finished, we were paid at the rate of £1 per day. The work was very light, merely consisting in removing clumps of toi-toi and Spaniards with sharp adzes, and cutting the scrub, flax, etc., with bill-hooks, the fern and small undergrowth being easily burnt the first hot sunny day.

About this time a strange incident occurred, which strikingly exemplified the words, "The race is not to the swift, nor the battle to the strong." My mate and I had arrived one afternoon on the south bank of the Buller, snd hoisted an old pair of trousers on the Maori flag-staff, as a signal for a canoe to come over for us from the township. It was during the vernal

equinox, and there was a high spring tide; and there
had been a vast amount of rain falling for some days,
so that the river was higher than I had yet seen it.
A perfect hurricane was blowing in from the sea, bringing the tide, which was already near its full, far up the
swollen waters of the river. While we were waiting
we heard a " cooing " to our left, in the direction from
which we had originally come from the Grey River, and
presently a number of men appeared coming towards
us in twos and threes; one with no trousers, another
with only a shirt and trousers, and all more or less de-
ficient as to wardrobe. They proved to be the passengers and crew of the " Gipsey," a small vessel that
had for some time been running between Nelson and
the Buller River, and which had just been wrecked a
few miles to the south. They soon joined us, and as
we all stood awaiting on the beach, we saw Mr. Skete
and others launching from the opposite shore the little
canoe in which Rowley and I had so often worked. It
was a small boat, so that with those already in it there
was scarcely room safely for more than two or three, but
so anxious were those ship-wrecked men to get to the
township, that five got into the canoe, besides taking
some of the baggage they had brought with them.
Rowley and I stayed behind with the rest and watched
the voyage of the canoe. A heavy sea was running,
partly from the force of the wind on the water of the
river, and partly from the high spring-tide meeting the
strong current. When half way over, a bigger wave
than usual broke into the canoe, but she righted again

and went on a few yards further, when a second wave knocked her clean over, and sent all hands under the water. We could see Mr. Skete's long body clinging to one end of the canoe, and one or two others doing the same, but the rest we could not distinguish. When we went over a short time afterwards, we found that they all had been saved with the exception of two; one of these had gained a champion medal for swimming in Sydney, and the other was considered one of the best swimmers in the Wellington Province, of which he was a native. He had frequently swam across the Buller before this with perfect ease. One of the saved, a tall young fellow, six feet high, told me that till that day he had never swam a stroke in his life, but, keeping his presence of mind, and remembering what little he had heard about swimming, he had kept his arms moving steadily on the water, and had thus kept himself afloat for more than twenty minutes, till a Maori canoe which had put out to the rescue picked him up. This is one amongst numerous cases which go to prove of how little avail the knowledge of swimming is in the New Zealand rivers, there being so very many under currents, besides boulders, snags, etc., which render them peculiarly dangerous, even to the best swimmer.

CHAPTER VI.

AND now Rowley and I parted for the first time for many months with much regret, at least on my side. He went up to the Lyell Creek, while I returned to the old Waimangaroa, as I had a liking for the place and wished to give it a good trial. Here I joined a party of three who occupied one of the old huts which had been built by some of the former population on the creek. One of these was a delightful fellow, who had sold out of the 25th some years before, and, though once a captain always a captain, was now a digger. Witty, good-natured (though a little hasty), hard-working, and a famous carpenter, he was as good a mate as any man could wish for in the bush where such qualities are invaluable, and we got, on very well together during the seven or eight months that we were mates. *En passant*, no class of men in the world are less generally known and appreciated than the digger. In saying this, I do not for one moment refer to those curses of a gold-field, the low Irish "tips," for a more cowardly, ruffianly, or brutal character I have never met with than that lively specimen from the green isle, who seems to flourish with rank luxuriance in the neighbourhood of gold. He is the man who will, as long as he has a mob of his mates to back him, smash up a store, jump a claim, rob a church, or shoot a gallant and inoffensive young prince, with equal zest. These are not the class to whom I refer as diggers. The true digger, whether Irish, Scotch, or English, is a brave, high-spirited working-man, ready with his purse as a friend, or with his fist as a foe. The dash of peril which necessarily accompanies the pursuits in which he is so constantly engaged imparts a free and careless bluffness to his manner, which is a great relief from the reserve and formality that prevail among nearly all classes in the old country. I know no more hospitable individual, in the full sense of the word, than this honest, jolly, free-hearted spendthrift. A share of his damper and bacon, or whatever else he may have, a pannikin of tea, or half his blanket and opossum rug, are always at your disposal if you choose to accept them. He on his part would, if compelled to seek it, expect to find the same welcome at your tent door, and would recall the kindness afterwards with gratitude, while endeavouring in every way to make you some return. *Mais revenons a nos moutons.*

We did nothing brilliant in the ground we had set into. We were driving through some ground below the hut, though we used to say that, as soon as we reached a spot exactly under our fire place, we should reach the gold. Meantime, the winter set in, so I determined to explore the ranges at the head of the Waimangaroa. Before doing so, however, Harrison and I ascended the range one morning to see what the country looked like on the top. This took so many hours that it was late in the day before we arrived at the top of the range above our " wharry." So many

spurs of the range branched off downwards in the
direction of the creek bed below, that it was a matter
of difficulty to find the particular one by which we had
ascended; but just as it began to get dark we caught
sight of one or two of our signs (twigs of small scrub
bent downwards or broken, so as to shew the lower
surfaces of the leaf, which, being of a lighter green than
the upper side, were seen in clear relief against the
darker tints surrounding them.)　Darker and darker it
became as we descended, the undergrowth as well as
the large timber increasing in density, so that, by the
time we had made our way some two hundred yards or
so downwards, we could not see our hands within a few
inches of our faces.　It had been raining all day, but
the night was cold and clear, and this, with our slow
progress, began to chill the very marrow of our bones.
We had neither of us any clothing beyond a light shirt
and trousers (Harrison having a waistcoat in addition),
which, wringing wet as they were, almost froze on our
bodies.　Still we went on foot by foot, feeling our
way with sticks, while at times the spur of the hill
was so narrow as to admit of only one at a time
advancing along it; and we knew that all the ravines
around were full of landslips, rocks, and waterfalls.
We felt our way carefully on, step by step, till we
came to a dead halt, as with our saplings we could
touch no bottom anywhere; so we sat down on a rotten
trunk, tired out, and with the pleasant prospect of
spending the night in a soaking bush, with feet and
hands benumbed with cold.　This, too, after a long day

spent in travelling over a rough country, with no
food since we left the hut in the morning. Luckily
I had two or three pieces of "nigger-head" tobacco
(Barrett's twist) in my pocket, and we chewed this as
we sat crouching back to back, shivering like a couple
of palsied rabbits. In spite of our situation sleepiness
came over us now and then, and we had to jump up
every ten minutes and go through what used to be
called "cabman's exercise." In this way we passed a
couple of wretched hours, till, agreeing that almost any
risk was better than this state of things, we determined
to hazard an attempt to reach some lower ground. We
accordingly tried all around us carefully, but without
success, till I suggested tying the two sticks together.
This done, we touched firm footing about a dozen feet
below, and with much scrambling and risk to life and
limb—for the sides of the spur were sometimes perpendicular—we landed on the ledge we had felt from above,
and cautiously advanced once more. Thus we got a
good way down until we came to a spot which we
found the next morning to be the edge of a precipice
some thirty or forty feet in depth, and, finding that we
could touch nothing with three sticks joined together,
we resigned ourselves to the necessity of passing the few
remaining hours of the night where we were. It may
be imagined with what eagerness we sought to catch
the first glimmer on a leaf or tree that would signal
the coming light, and with what haste we made a
circuit round the dangerous brink upon which we had
been perched, and skedaddled to our "wharry." We

found our mates had visited the township in our absence for supplies of tucker, and had brought back with them some fresh beef, the first I had tasted for nearly a year.

We had found the whole of the ranges above almost bare of bush, patches of the manuka and coromica alone affording shelter and firewood for a camp, and coal-seams cropping out of the ground for miles. Having made up my mind to go up and camp among the ranges for a few weeks, I proposed that the party should square up accounts and divide the tucker, and whoever should strike anything good in the way of gold should let the rest know. This having been all arranged, I took a few days to patch clothes and mend an old tent, etc. I then took up my tent and blankets, my usual change of things, and ascended the range. I pitched the tent in the best patch of the tea-tree scrub I could find, making a bed-place, and a sod chimney at the door of the tent to sit at in the evenings, which, as the snow had already begun to fall, would be considerably chilly. Then, coming down again, I took fifty pounds of flour, a good hunch of salt beef, tea and sugar, billy, etc., with an old volume of "Household Words" to spell over at my little fire in the evenings by the light of my slush-lamp. The snow came down and almost shut me in, but for nearly a month I made the little tent my head-quarters, going out for a day or so at a time, and prospecting the different creeks and the head of the Waimangaroa itself, taking only a couple of blankets, my tools, tent, and a few cakes, and camping under rocks, and in all sorts of corners about the wild bed of the stream. The scenery was sometimes very grand. I do not think anything on the Swiss lakes or the Rhine could surpass it.

Finding no inducement to prolong my stay in the district I had traversed, I spent a day or two quietly in my snug little camp, enjoying the lovely scenery all round during the day, and my pipe and Dickens at at night in my chimney corner, and then made a start down again.

On my return to the lower world in the creek-bed, I found the party broken up, one having joined in a drive or tunnel, and the other two, Captain Harrison and "old Brookes," moved down to a little piece of ground which they intended to work quietly by them-themselves. "Old Brookes," though far advanced in life, was still a fine looking soldierly man ; he had served in the Life Guards in his earlier years, was a capital cook, a good manager in a rough party, and had a very high opinion of the "little captain," looking upon him as a prince in disguise, whose kingdom was one day to return to him.

At this juncture I was offered a piece of ground by a man up the creek who had got good gold out of it him-self, and was only leaving to go to some better ground up the Buller River. I took for a mate a fine fellow, a Lan-cashire coal-miner, and a first-rate workman. We had a good deal of blasting to do, and in this line he proved himself thoroughly well versed. There being

no good fuses to be obtained for blasting, he made
vesta matches answer equally well, using a "needle"
and "tamping" instead of the regular fuse. My former
mate, who was driving a tunnel a little above us, came
down to us more than once to get a hint from my chum
about the blasting, and this led, through the poor
fellow's own carelessness, to a sad accident, by which he
lost the sight of both his eyes. I was one day washing
a dish of stuff in the creek below the claim, when I
heard a shout above, and, looking up, saw the man
with whom he was working running down the track
with a face like a ghost, calling for help. I immediately ran up and passed him—for he was too flabber-
gasted to speak a word beyond "blast," "blown up,"
"dead man"—and on reaching the drive found poor
Ned crawling out from beneath it on all fours, and
with a face like a plum pudding. He seemed to know
at once the full extent of the mischief, for his first words
were, "I wish to God it had killed me ; I shall be blind
for life!" I got him down to our hut, and next day,
with the help of his mate, took him down the creek,
which was no easy work, for there was no way but
over high rocks, precipices, thick bush, etc., and crossing
the river itself continually till we reached its mouth,
where a dray was in waiting that we had sent for to
take him to the Buller township. I stayed with him
and nursed him for a week, poor fellow ; but I knew
from the first that it was a lost case as regarded his
eyes. At the end of that time I returned to my claim
and never saw him more ; shortly after he was sent up

to Nelson, where he was taken to a hospital, and I believe that everything was done that could have been for his benefit, but to no avail. Such are the chances and dangers of this sort of life, from which I, on looking back and remembering the many " I have seen around me fall," feel deeply thankful that I was preserved. Nowhere is sympathy more ready or more substantial than among the community of a gold-field. A subscription was raised immediately, which paid for his expenses to Nelson, and left him a good sum in hand for necessary expenses when he arrived there. I trust he has since learnt that it was the hand of God which seemed so heavy at the time, and has perhaps even rejoiced at the chastening.

I worked with "Lanky" for a month, during which time we did very fairly, though the work was both difficult and dangerous, being a drive or tunnel made into the side of the hill, or rather cliff, blasting the rocks that were too big to get out otherwise, and going in underneath the hill without using any props, which are generally used in drives to support the weight overhead. At the end of this time, as my mate had steady work offered him, I determined to try another expedition over the ground I had gone over before, and went down to the township to obtain stores and look for a mate. I found two sawyers who had been doing well at their trade for some time past, but were out of work at this time, who were delighted at the idea of joining me in one of my mountain wanderings. We soon made our preparations and started. Although during the few weeks we were engaged in this expedition we had no discovery of anything payable in the way of gold, we yet enjoyed the trip very much. My mates were both religious men, and as they were the only specimens of that description that I met during all the years of my nomadic life, I shall ever remember them and their kindly qualities. They had neither of them seen much of real bush-roughing before, and I used to enjoy a good laugh every night and morning at the peculiar apparitions they presented with their heads wrapped in white night-caps as they sang a hymn of Wesley's before turning either in or out of their opossum rugs. They were real good fellows, and I hope they will be successful in whatever they may undertake.

I came back from this stroll in a tattered old flanne shirt not bigger than a waistcoat, and a flour-bag with a couple of holes in it in place of my trousers, which had been burned while left to dry over the fire after a soaking day in the bush. But the denizens of the Buller River in those days were by no means critical as to " costume." " Chacun a son gout " was the prevailing motto, and a postage stamp and a shirt collar might have been safely adopted by any one of airy notions as a neat and inexpensive mode of dress. This last disappointment gave me rather a disgust to the place, and I determined to go back to civilization for a time, and become once more a victim of tailors' bills. With this intention I paid all that I could afford at the time to the various storekeepers to whom I was

F

indebted, and, with a hearty shake of the hand from each of them and my own chums, I went up to Nelson by the "Sturt" steamer, *en route* to Canterbury. I put up at the Trafalgar "à la digger," and spent a week very pleasantly in trotting about Nelson, and riding up and down in the omnibus from the wharf into the town and back again. This latter amusement may seem childish, but to one who had not seen anything beyond a Sydney dray for nearly two years, and that only occasionally, the luxury of motion in an easy carriage, moving swiftly along on a tramway, was very enjoyable, and not to be wondered at.

After a few days' rest I packed my swag and started in a trap that took me about twenty miles out of town to a place called by the strange title of Fox Hill, if I remember right ; from the inn at which place, after a capital dinner and lots of cream and fruit, I set out on my way overland to Canterbury, a distance of nearly two hundred miles, with rivers of large size to be crossed, which, if swelled by rain, would delay me perhaps for days. At this time there were five accommodation houses between Nelson and Christchurch, though I have no doubt by this time there are many more. I had exactly £2 and a few shillings to carry me this distance, and I trudged off with a light heart, making about ten miles before the afternoon began to wear. I generally stopped to drink at every creek I came to, and, having done so on this occasion, I was feeling in my pocket, as I got up from the ground at one of these creeks, to make sure that my little store of wealth was

safe, when, to my horror and consternation, I found
that the two £1 notes were gone, leaving only the
silver, which would scarcely carry me beyond the next
house of call, at the prices then charged for everything.
I at once conceived I must have dropped them while
stopping to drink or to rest, so I walked back a distance
of eight miles the same evening to a small wayside
shanty, close to a narrow belt of bush that I had
passed a mile or two after setting out. The landlord was a digger who had made a small "pile," and,
having married, had started this house for travellers.
He seemed to doubt the yarn I spun, as was very
natural ; so I contented myself with a pint of beer
before I turned in, feeling that supper was not to be
thought of under the circumstances. In the morning
I took another pint, and, having rolled up my blankets
and got my swag in order, was preparing for rather a
spiritless trudge, when the landlord, who had hitherto
said nothing, asked me if I had searched the bush
track leading from his shanty to the inn from whence I
had started. I said I had not, but that I would do so
if he would keep an eye on my swag. He agreed, and
away I went, looking into corner after corner where I
thought I had been before. At last, just as I was giving
up the search, I came suddenly on a little opening in
the bush beside the track where I remembered waiting
for a few minutes, and on casting my eyes round I saw
my two scraps of notes lying curled up together in the
dew. Affectionately did I gather them into my bosom,
and swiftly did I return unto "mine host," who

straightway produced "pasty and sack" for my refreshment, and sent me rejoicing on my way.

It came on to rain just after I entered a bush called "Ten Mile Bush," and I began to look round for a place of shelter for the night. At the edge of the track lay a "length" of a felled tree, quite five feet through, and perfectly hollow, though closed up with earth and roots at the further end. This I cleaned out, and, spreading my blankets inside, sat down contentedly enough by the fire while my billy was boiling for tea. Two horsemen came by while I was waiting, and tried in vain to persuade me to go back to the last station with them to sleep.

It rained hard all night and all next day, so that by the time I got to the creek running into the Wairau, up which river the track led, it had swollen to a torrent, and, there being no bridge, I was as well off as a waggoner at a turnpike, with the gate shut and no money in his pocket.

Seeing that there was no help for it, I made the best of a bad thing and put up a "mi-mi" for the night; but it was something like sleeping under the spray of a fountain.

Next morning I went up the creek in search of a place to get over, and found some way up a couple of saplings, about six inches in diameter, that had been laid in the forks of two trees that hung slightly over the bank on each side of the stream; a shepherd was crossing with his two dogs as I reached the spot. Though my heavy swag was wet through and through, I managed to reach the opposite bank in safety, and a few miles further on arrived at a hut on a cattle station, where I was agreeably surprised to find an old man and boy engaged in concocting a rabbit-stew for dinner. There were no means of crossing the Wairau except by swimming, and this I objected to on many accounts ; so, making myself as comfortable as I could, and whiling away the time with rabbit hunting among the rocks, I waited at the hut for two days.

On the third morning a horseman passed, and very kindly offered me a lift over on the saddle behind him. I was soon trudging away along the winding bridle track which wound up the gorge, and chatting with my "carrier." He was one of the owners of Tarndale, the largest cattle station in the country, and the next day I passed the homestead, and saw a party of his hands preparing for a mustering expedition.

After a night spent at a rough sort of accommodation house on the Clarence River, I started over "Jolly's Pass," which separates the Wairau country from the Hanmer Plains, and over which I had a most onjoyable walk, though the sun was very oppressive. A bite of damper and a pannikin of beer sent me on to the Waiho River, which I reached in the evening. Here I found a Mr. Handyside, with a party of men, preparing to throw a suspension bridge across the river at the height of, I think, 300 feet above the water from cliff to cliff. They had advanced no further than the foundations on either side at the time I arrived, and I found that I should have to travel over on two or three boards nailed together, which slender carriage, attached to a couple of strong ropes, was drawn backwards and forwards by pulleys. To get on to this concern I had to do "Blondin" for four or five yards, which performance being my first of the kind, and my heavy swag rendering me too hampered to balance myself easily, I was more than delighted when I found myself once more on *terra firma.* Mr. Handyside, the architect and engineer of the bridge, very kindly gave me a "shakedown" and a good feed, and the next morning I started on all the fresher.

The rest of the road being comparatively unrelieved by any feature of interest, I will go on to Christchurch, where I enjoyed a real spell of what diggers call a "paper-collar life ;" but, as usual, after that length of time, I began to want a change, and bethought me whither next to turn my steps.

CHAPTER VII.

ISAPPOINTED so severely on the diggings, I began to think of my old trade of soldiering, and, having good introductions in the north, I took my passage in a coasting steamer, " The Queen," whose commander, Captain Francis, was as jovial and good-hearted a little skipper as ever trod a bridge, and, after touching at Nelson, Wellington and Taranaki, arrived at at the Manukau Heads in safety.

Here, after a few days, I presented my papers, which were pronounced satisfactory by the then War Minister, and I was told that I could place my name at the bottom of the list if I chose (it already contained upwards of 100 names), and take my chance of a commission in the honourable (?) Colonial Army ! I declined, feeling at once that my chance was indeed minute. Next day I saw a boy of less than twenty, who was said to have been turned out of the navy, gazetted to a commission a few days after his arrival in the colony, and a short time afterwards he was seen on the march, in command of a detachment of Waikato Militia, drunk, and rolling along the road at the head of his men, arm and arm with a. sailor with whom he had chummed. What I say on this matter I say not from any soreness on my part, but from an unprejudiced view of the then existing system of things at the seat of Government. I saw at that time men walking the streets of Auckland, adventurers certainly, and soldiers of fortune,

but yet men who had served half their lives in half
the countries in the world, whose claims were ignored
by the money-lending Methodist who had at that time
the control of affairs ; while the last sweeping of an
aristocratic dunghill, or the nephew (as in the case of
the child I mentioned above) of a " great Mogul," were
he the most worthless and inexperienced character conceivable, would have his claims allowed.   The attempt
at any denial of these charges would be utterly useless
in the face of facts which can be produced, for they are
notoriously well known to all who have had a private
view "behind the scenes."

I must mention here a trivial incident that becomes
interesting at the time I am writing, when the death of
Major Von Tempsky in the field has just appeared in
the papers.   That gallant soldier was at this time in
Auckland, holding the rank of Captain, and in the very
zenith of his reputation, being deservedly made a lion
of ; for a more fearless and dashing officer has never
served in the Colonial or any other army.

I had gone one day to the War Office, and was waiting in the anteroom for an interview with Mr B——,
the Minister.   One or two persons had also entered
after me ; one of them was Captain Von Tempsky.
His appearance, though slightly too melodramatic, was
wild and picturesque : a rough, blue serge shirt, open
at the breast, over which his long black hair fell flowing over his shoulders, clear cut features, which, though
seamed and worn with a reckless and hazardous life, were
still handsome.   In short, he was more like one of Salva-

tor Rosa's brigands than a commissioned officer in the
nineteenth century. He, as well as the rest of us, was
waiting till our turns should come to see the Minister.
Some time passed without the summons being given.
At length the attendant came to say that Mr. B—— was
at leisure. There was an immediate advance of more than
one, when Captain Von Tempsky stepped before the rest,
with a bow, and asserted his right to enter, his business
being of extreme and urgent importance ; then turning
attention to me, he observed, " And if it were not so,
this young gentleman has a claim prior to all of us,
having waited the longest for an interview, so I shall
beg to waive my right in his favour, if he will permit
me." I insisted on his seeing Mr. B—— before me, as
his business was of far more importance than my
own, and, after a few courteous refusals, gained my
point.

About this time I made the acquaintance of one who,
like many other of my colonial friends, was a strange
anomaly. He had been many things in his time, and
was now full private in the 3rd Waikato Regiment of
Militia. He had come down to Auckland, on a short
leave of absence, to meet a brother who was about to
sail for England, to take possession of a legacy of
£30,000. This young brother had himself come up from
Wellington in the steamer with me, and by him I was
introduced to my mad friend, and also to another private
of the same regiment who had come down with Duncan.
Him, after a short conversation. I found to be the son
of a Devonshire vicar, and from the neighbourhood of

some of my own relatives. With these two mad-caps
for my Poins and Bardolph, I dropped a most unpro-
fitable fortnight into the lap of time; then, having
received change for my last piece of paper, I began to
contemplate a move.

Being one day in the neighbourhood of the Club
House, I heard that the doctor of the —rd regiment (a
detachment of which was then stationed at the Lower
Wairoa) was about to sail round to that place in a
small boat. Having a cousin in the regiment, I introduced myself to the worthy medico, and was immediately offered a " lift " in his little craft. We had a
most merry passage, just arriving in time for the mess
in their snug "wharry." Among the officers in the
detachment was a big and intensely comical Irishman,
whose flirtations with the Maori beauties of the neighbourhood were a source of constant amusement. He
thoroughly believed that they understood the richness
of his brogue, and would " bother " them as if they were
regular Connemara darlings, though to all his overtures
their only answer was a volley of gutturals that would
have put to the rout the impudence of any but a
Paddy.

After a few days thus spent, I proceeded to a place in
the neighbourhood, where was stationed part of the
Colonial Defence Force, a mounted corps, to the officers
of which my cousin had given me letters of introduction. Through the interest of these and my own recommendation as a fair rider, I was before long enrolled
as an orderly attached to the gallant C. D. F. s.

Of these orderlies (they were twenty-five in number) eleven were born and bred as gentlemen ; one was a claimant in an interminable peerage case, pending the settlement of which Private Tracy was content to be the D'Orsay of a colonial troop of cavalry. Another was an Irish lawyer, whose relatives had been eminent in various branches of that profession in their native country for centuries. We employed the best tailor, bootmaker and hatter in the town of Auckland. Our duties consisted in attending stables three times a day, in keeping our revolvers and saddlery bright and clean, our boots without a speck to dim their polish, our breeches neat and in good order, and the broad white bands of our little cavalry caps in a perpetual condition of pipeclay. Beyond this, reading the papers when off duty in the verandah of the neighbouring hotel, criticising the coach passengers that stopped there for refreshment, and flirting with the settlers' daughters, was our sole employment. At the end of six months, the war being for the most part at an end, it was suddenly discovered by Government that the Postal Orderlies, though a highly ornamental body of men, were scarcely indispensable to the wellbeing and safety of the community at large ; accordingly, on a pleasant and sunshiny morning, we were quietly discharged from further service, and I dropped at once from the get-up of a spur-clanking trooper into the unpretending garments of a private citizen.

A few days later, I was sitting at a desk in the Commissary-General's office on the Fort Hill, performing

the duties of an extra clerk attached thereto, with the
style and title of lance-sergeant. The pressure of business, which had been the cause of my appointment, however, being shortly withdrawn, I, with others in a like
case, was soon pronounced a free man again, that freedom
slightly clogged with the loss of three-and-sixpence a
day and rations. Things about this time began to wear
an unpromising appearance, and were soon at their
worst, when, after three days of existence supported
solely by five carraway biscuits, a pint of beer, and all
the water-cress I could consume from the public gardens, I had serious thoughts of a raid on a beef and
ham shop, the proprietor of which had refused me a
plate of meat. Affairs when in this state are generally
pronounced "sure to mend." I at this juncture received a satisfactory answer from my kind-hearted
cousin to whom I had applied for a helping hand.
Another week passed away, and I was still as far as
ever from obtaining the certainty of three meals a day.
I had gone over to Onehunga one afternoon to answer
an advertisement for a substitute in the Waikato
Militia, which offered as a bonus the munificent sum of
£5. When coming away disappointed as usual (for
there had been over forty applications for the same
thing), I observed one applicant of more refined manner and appearance than the rest walking slowly and
despondingly away. Bringing up alongside of him, I
hailed him in colonial parlance with the usual saluta-
tion, "Well mate, what luck?" His reply was decidedly low-spirited, and our sympathies being mu-

tually awakened, we soon became confidential, and agreed to join forces.

On comparing notes as to the state of the funds, we ascertained that our combined resources amounted to exactly eighteenpence. Having now a partner in misfortune, I determined to go up the country and endeavour to obtain work for both of us on one of the farms. Before making a start I contrived to raise one pound by a lucky accident (not worth mentioning), and after a good feed, a good bed, and a good smoke, we took the road with spirits far lighter even than our pockets. A few days found us at Drury, again reduced to about ninepence in ready money, and a small loaf. My companion had with him the remnants of his *menage*, in the shape of a glossy white blanket. This I began to view with an eye to business, and suggested its immediate sale. My partner agreeing, I straightway carried it on my arm to the nearest store, where, after a quarter of an hour's hard bargaining with the buxom mistress of the establishment, I succeeded in disposing of it for eight shillings. This sum we expended in sufficient flour, tea, and sugar to keep our bodies and souls together for at least a day or two.

On entering the township we had noticed at the side of the road a small thatched hut, of which we now took possession, and while Finnerty mixed the flour in the hut, I borrowed an axe from some brickmakers close by, and went into the bush for firewood. Having cut a sufficient quantity, we "humped" it out of the bush and packed it beside our new home. The weather

was very cold, and as we had no warm coverings we
were obliged to range ourselves close in front of a large
fire at which we baked our bread.   In this way,
travelling the country by day in search of work,
and returning at night to our hut, we passed some
days while our supplies lasted.   During the evenings
spent over our pipes, gazing into the red logs in front of
us, I drew from Finnerty the circumstances that had
brought him to this pass.   His history was rather
curious.   But four months before this time a lieutenant
in the 7—th, he had the command of an Imperial Chinese
regiment under Major Gordon, and while in that position had seen good service in the field.   The only trousers
he had left had more than one shot hole in them, good
proof of his having smelt powder in their company.
Unfortunately fond of the speculative excitement attached to the turf, he had come down with nearly
eighteen months' extra salary (£100 per month command allowance) to the Hong Kong races, and had
" stood to win " a considerable amount.

As it has happened to many a poor fellow before, he
lost beyond all possibility of payment, except by the
sale of his commission.   On the evening of that day of
losses he sat down and " sent in his papers," taking care,
however, to state that he did so for the express purpose
of settling in New Zealand.   This proviso entitled him
to the possession of 400 acres within the province of
Auckland.   His resignation accepted and his debts
paid, he came straight to Auckland, his small stock of
ready money having been soon exhausted, swallowed

up by the capacious maw of a colonial lodging-house keeper. He had sought for employment of any description ; in this he had utterly failed.

In the middle of one night we were roused by a roaring in our ears, and had only time, the one to snatch his pocket-book (containing the land order referred to) from the thatch, the other his black "dudheen" from the same place, before the hut was a raging furnace. We had kept ourselves too warm that night.

Once more houseless, with only one small cake left, we set out on our travels. With alternate good and bad luck we journeyed on, and in a few days found ourselves back in Auckland. With a feeling of desperation we entered a good hotel and took rooms. After breakfast in the morning we went into the town with the same old object in view. The first place to which the "hard-up" were wont to betake themselves at that hour was the office of the *Southern Cross* newspaper, in the advertisement sheet of which, pasted up outside, they would seek for a chance of congenial billets. While peering over the heads of the mixed mob there as usual collected, we spied among the "wanted" an' advertisement for a substitute in the Waikato Militia. The bonus offered was £20, and as Finnerty had the longest legs I packed him off to the address of the advertiser. Seeing nothing better for myself than the chance of a boatman's place at Wynyard Pier, I was hurrying in that direction, when, on turning the corner of Shortland Crescent, I was met by a worthy sergeant of my acquaintance, who greeted

me with words of startling effect: " Money, you're the
very man I have been hunting for for days ; you've
come in for a lot of money." The news was true as
welcome; the subsidy from home placed me in position.
The tide had turned, and after once more arraying myself in decent attire I took ship and went to Christchurch.

On my arrival I went up the country to stay with
my old friend Collison, the co-editor of our paper on
the voyage out. His father having died shortly before
and left him some thousands, he had bought land and
settled on it, doing most of the labouring work himself.
I found him snugly established in a boarded cabin, with
a good shingle roof above, while at a short distance
from it were a stable and tool house, with a hut for
any men he might have occasion to employ. The inside of his den was a complete little bachelor's hall.
Two book-cases filled with books hung on the wall;
two neat iron bedsteads, one at each side of the room;
with table, wash-stand, chairs, and a few trunks, completed the furniture of the apartment, which I shared
with him for three delightful weeks.

The accounts of my wanderings upon the West
Coast soon spread far and wide, and amongst others
infected by them with a spirit of adventure was a man
of wiry constitution and active habits employed in the
neighbourhood with a party of surveyors. He offered
to give up his situation, and share the chances of my
next trip to the diggings. These were situated on the
very creek at which we had landed from our "mogueys"

after our flying voyage down the Teremakau. A few miles above the place we had then worked on there had since been found a good payable gold-field, and to this we were now bound. On our arrival we procured a tent, tools, and tucker, pegged off a claim, and were soon hard at work.

A month passed with varying success, during which we tried more than one piece of ground. The only event worth mentioning during our stay on the Green-stone Creek was the discovery, by two old Buller diggers of my acquaintance, of a huge lump of greenstone, the largest that had yet been found in the islands. We saw it in their claim (which was on a terrace some fifty feet above the creek) the morning after its discovery. The size of the greenstone was from 18 inches to 2 feet in width, and about $2\frac{1}{2}$ feet in height ; its surface was smooth as glass, and when struck with a pick or a stone it gave out a metallic ring. It was sold subsequently to the Maories for £10.

At the end of a month we resolved on a change. Accordingly we tossed up one Sunday morning which of the creeks we should make for. The lot fell on one with the arithmetical title of the Six-mile Creek, from which good accounts had been arriving for some time. A mile or two from the beach on the edge of this creek we came the next day on a small flock of storekeepers on the wing for the central point of the diggings some twelve miles up the river. Great news had lately arrived, and a tremendous rush was expected to set in. Naturally wishing to be the first at the scramble, we

G

hurried on. By the time we had boiled our billy, at
daw-dawn the next morning, outside the future township which we had reached overnight, we were surrounded by an eager mob — lighting fires, pitching
tents, drinking, fighting, cursing, and shouting, all at
once. By eleven o'clock, in the heart of a dense and
almost untrodden bush, a street had arisen as if created
by the magic wand of an enchanter. Swift as the
walls of Aladdin's palace, stores, shanties, public-
houses, butchers, bakers, and doctors' shops, were to be
found on every side; while in the thick of the densely-
packed throng that filled the roadway from one end to
the other I counted no less than three ring fights, carried
on most energetically by both principals and backers.
We spent that day and the next in rushing up the
branches of the Six-mile, but found every inch of
ground occupied. Returning rather despondingly in
the evening, we determined to wait no longer amongst
the crowd, but to strike out over the head of the range
in search of fresh ground. Here we were again disappointed, for what little was worth trying was already
taken up. We were returning to the Six-mile, when I
heard voices hailing me from the top of a hill above
me. Looking up, I saw some Maories, whom I had
known on the Buller River, beckoning to me. Seeing
there was something in the wind, I coo'ed to my mate,
and tumbled up the rise as fast as I could. With them
I found Bill Everest, who had been one of my party
down the old Teremakau. "You're right, old man,"
said he, as I came up panting; "follow the signs

through there," pointing to the bush, "and they will take you to Maori Gully."

I had heard a vague whisper of a "find" called by this name during the morning ; but, as these things are always kept a profound secret, I had despaired of learning the situation. Into the bush I dashed without a word, and for some miles, alternately losing and finding the "spoor," in the shape of trodden undergrowth and broken twigs, arrived late in the evening at the foot of a spur, at a spot overhanging the creek of which I was in search. On looking over the edge of the ravine I saw below me the faces of several that I had known on the Greenstone. They had evidently arrived but a very short time, and were shouldering their swags after descending the ugly-looking drop between us. By letting our swags fall with a run, and throwour tools after them, we were enabled to make a breakneck descent into the creek below ; and an hour afterwards were crowing over our luck at being among the favoured few destined to make their "piles" in Maori Gully. Alas for the vanity of human expectations and the patchy character of New Zealand gold-fields! our claim proved a "duffer." No less than fifteen shafts did we sink in the terrace and creek within the limits of our claim, but found a prospect of nothing sufficient to encourage us in working it. Disgusted with our bad fortune, we resolved to separate, I myself taking the remainder of our provisions, and with one mate going out for a fortnight's prospecting. At the end of that time, finding no encouragement, I returned to the Six-mile township, resolving to take the first job I came across. I had not been in the place many hours before I was appointed assistant to a baker, with a salary of £4 a week, my board, and as many meat-pies and as much hop-beer as I could contrive to consume. My duties must have slightly differed, I conceive, from those attached to the same office in this country. I had to keep two large ovens constantly supplied with firewood, which I had to fall, split, and carry out of the bush. Besides this, I brought the water, necessary for the large quantity of bread which my employer supplied to the community of storekeepers and diggers, from the creek. Chopping the beef for pies, making hop-beer, and cooking our meals, besides taking my turn in the shop, occupied what little remained of my day. Night was devoted to playing euchre, cribbage or all-fours, or to yelling convivial choruses and dancing to the tune of a stray fiddle. A month slipped away, and my "boss" found his business so increase as to enable him to establish branch bakeries on other creeks in the neighbourhood. This requiring additional capital, he took to himself a partner for the management of the Six-mile trade. Not liking this change in the administration, I gave up office, merely remarking, what was afterwards verified, that the new manager would require two hands to do my work.

I next turned my attention to chimney-building, and contracted with a neighbouring storekeeper to erect him a wide and substantial fire-place, the chimney included, 9 feet in height, for £5. I employed an assistant at £1 a-day, and in two days we finished the chimney. Home readers must not picture to themselves a solid brick edifice such as is generally associated with their ideas of a chimney. The apparatus that I employed in its construction was simple in the extreme ; it consisted solely of from twenty to thirty straight limbs 12 feet long, a few hand-barrow loads of large stones, and a few buckets full of mud. A bullock's hide stretched round the top made the sides sufficiently air-tight to allow of a clear vent. My first undertaking having succeeded beyond my expectations, I had orders soon for as many chimneys as I could erect, and as I seldom cleared less than two pounds per day I considered it a lucrative profession. Other competitors, however, starting in the business, I had to turn my attention to something else. The stores and public-houses having been put upon uneven ground, I contracted also to level the floors in their interior, and subsequently laid down gravel thereon. This also for a time was a paying game ; but before many weeks demand for labour of this description began to fail, and consequently for some days I was thrown out of work. At this time the road from the beach up to the township, a distance of twelve miles, passing, as it did, the whole way through heavy bush and thick undergrowth, and crossing and re-crossing the creek-bed every hundred yards, was in a condition perfectly inconceivable to those who have not been to a great rush on the West Coast Diggings in New Zealand. Roots of all sizes, torn and mangled when small into a sort of maccaroni squash, and when large remaining a dead hindrance to both horses and man, caused the mud ploughed by cattle and pack-horses to assume the appearance of a torrent; so bad was it that the whole distance was marked by the bones of dead animals. The price given for the package of stores was £3 per hundred for the twelve miles, and I suddenly bethought me of the possibility of making myself into a very profitable pack-horse.

Turning into the nearest store accordingly, I called for a nobbler, and asked the storeman, while he bittered the decoction, what he would give a man for bringing the various articles he required.

He stared on hearing my question, and said, "Why, you're never going to make a beast of burden of yourself, mate, are you?"

I replied that I would make any sort of "beast" of myself if the remuneration were only sufficient.

He said, "Well, old man, you bring me the goods, and I'll pay you the same as the hosses."

"Done," said I. "What are you wanting up most at this time?"

"Well," said the storekeeper, "I've had a run on my picks, so you can bring as many of them as you like, though they're not a lively lot to carry about, and I should fancy would give a man a crick in the back. There's a little keg of rum waiting for me down at the beach, so you can make up a load the best way you can."

I found the keg awkward enough, but the picks were

altogether too lively to carry far. After working the skin off the small of my back I left them half way, and completed my journey with the rum cask. Next day, in place of wood and iron, I shouldered a 50 lb. bag of flour, and did the distance comfortably, earning thereby thirty shillings. I continued to carry from 50 to 70 lbs. for some days, always increasing little by little the weight of my load. As this was the first time such a thing had been attempted on those diggings, I had to undergo a tremendous fire of "Joes" from every chum I passed. The word "Joe" expresses the derision usually bestowed on new chums on the diggings, or any man acting, or dressing, or speaking in any way considered as *outré* by the diggers themselves. "He laughs who wins," and, as I knew many who thus jeered were glad to get a pound a day by even harder work than I was doing for double the money, I could afford to laugh with them. After three weeks' practice, having become known as "Charley the Packer," I had plenty of orders to carry up every description of store; from tea and gin-cases to soap and salt fish; and seldom after that did I shoulder less than 100 lbs. Times getting dull about the Six-mile, I was joined one by one by many others, several of whom had been among the first to "Joe" me at the beginning. Never having strained myself beyond my powers, I did not feel any ill effects from the heavy labour I underwent, though 100 lbs. was a weight which very few cared to attempt on such a track. Two men who had taken to this means of gaining their livelihood fell

victims of their ambition, for, instead of commencing
with the calf and ending with the bull as I had done,
they staggered under the full weight of 100 lb. bags of
flour, sugar, etc., till their strength gave way and their
coffins had to be prepared for them. A day or two
after the demise of one of these poor fellows, I took a
bag of flour to Charlie McLeod, the storekeeper, who,
being a carpenter by trade, did duty when required as
an undertaker.

As I dropped my load inside the door, Charlie looked
up from his hammering, and, eyeing it where it lay,
said, pointing to his work : " Thought one was enough,
but I guess I'll want your measure, old hoss, before
long ;" and he believed it too.

The novelty of this occupation, however, soon ceased,
and I left my quarters at Mo' Thomas's (a distinguished member of the P. R.), where I had been staying for some weeks, and determined to try the effect of
change of air on the sea coast. Accordingly, I, with my
blankets, made my appearance in the streets of Hokitika, a town then in its infancy.   While remaining here
a day or two I heard that Dr. H———, the provincial
conchologist, required some one or two, with a knowledge of the bush and West Coast travelling, to ac-
company him on a tour of inspection over the diggings.
The wages offered were trifling, but as I was curious to
see what equivalent was obtained by Government for
the £1,500 a year which constituted his salary, I hitched
on. We were three in party besides the doctor, one
being a Maori who carried the blankets, clothes, and

entire paraphanalia of the worthy *savant*, together
with his own swag. For the short time during which
I accompanied this gentleman, I cannot affirm that he
was other than liberal in his conduct, but I confess our
first day's dinner struck me as too much on the "do
the boys" principle to be a pleasant precedent to our
future condition. On arrival at old Mo's shanty, my
late abode, which lay in our road, it was about dinner
time. This I suggested to Dr. H——, who accordingly directed that the billy should be put on the fire
in Mo's shanty, "and," said he, pulling out a two-
shilling piece, "as we use his fire we may as well buy
our provisions for our dinner from him ; this will get a
box of sardines, which will be more than enough for
our small party." I could not help laughing as I described to Mo the grand air with which our German
"boss" tendered the price of two nobblers for the purchase of four men's dinners. The doctor's mode of
travelling was by no means laborious. Well clothed
and booted, with a cigar in his mouth, he toddled, or
rather rolled, along with a pompous air, stopping occasionally to inspect the washing of a dish, or to turn
over the gravel heaps of stuff with the end of his stick.
A fortnight of this sort of thing satisfied me with regard to the onerous responsibilities devolving on so im-
portant a personage as the provincial conchologist, and
I returned to Christchurch, norrowly escaping being
snowed up on the dividing range by the way.

CHAPTER VIII.

SHORTLY after my arrival in Christchurch I was called upon at my hotel by a gentleman who had found a new track over the ranges to Hokitika, the chief town on the West Coast diggings. He came to ask me to join a party with which he proposed in mid-winter to force a passage through the snow, which at that season covered the country for many miles on either side of the main range. It was with great regret that I refused Mr. Griffiths' offer ; but I had previously engaged to join another party, having the same end in view, under a surveyor, who was at that time high in the service of Government. This gentleman had shared with Mr. Griffiths in the discovery of the pass. Our departure caused some sensation at the time. A large-sized dray, loaded with tools, canvas, flour, meat, and necessaries of every description accompanied us, and under it, I, with two others, made my bed every night. Passing station after station, we arrived at length at the bed of a river covered with large boulders, along which it was impossible to take a dray. This river has its rise in a low saddle, over which our course lay, and we were now compelled to use pack saddles for the conveyance of our stores to the foot of the range. An event of a melancholy nature threw a gloom over the party on the first day after our arrival amongst the snow. One of the party, a fine, high-spirited young fellow, was going out duck shooting for the benefit of our larder. It was a sunny, clear morning, and he was preparing his ammunition within the tent when two Paradise ducks came in view, sailing over our heads. There was a general shout from all hands for Jenkins. "Now's your time, Jenkins." Out he rushed, gun in hand, and in his eagerness to view the quarry tripped over a tent rope at the door. The gun went off, sending the charge into the thigh of one of the party who was standing within two or three feet of him. We bound up the wound as well as we were able, and one of our party, a sailor, rigged up a sort of hammock, which we slung to a stout pole. In this we contrived, though with great difficulty, to carry him back through the rivers and snow to the last station we had passed. The poor fellow died in the hospital shortly afterwards ; he left a widow and several children, to whom Jenkins, who was terribly cut up by the event, made a present of £100, a large sum for him.

About a mile and a half from the foot of the pass we pitched our camp, and began to clear a spot in the snow for the erection of a slab hut. We cleared a space sufficient for a good-sized dwelling place, and then proceeded to fell and split the necessary timber, to obtain which we started into the bush at daylight every morning. Certainly, never before or since have I experienced the same torture from cold as during the hours spent in that frozen bush, every branch and leaf of which was covered with a coating of ice, before the sun's first weak rays came to mock us with a

semblance of warmth. A month or six weeks was spent
chiefly in this labour, though occasional attempts were
made to cut our way up the frozen side of the pass.
More than once we had reached a considerable distance
above the river bed, but on each occasion during the
night following the snow fell to such a depth as to fill
up the footway we had taken such pains to cut in the
ice with our sharp spades. A circumstance happened
at this time which forced us to adopt a different plan.
There had been a very severe frost one night, and by
the next afternoon we attained a height of some 800
feet of point blank elevation above the foot of the
pass. Mr. Browning was in advance of us, and I, as
usual on such expeditions, followed close behind him ;
behind me, dotted like flies along the sloping side of a
sugar loaf, were the rest of our own party, followed
by Mr. Parks and his party, in all some fourteen
hands. As we had only intended to reach on this day
an elevation sufficient to afford us a good survey of the
last and most difficult portion of our route, we had
brought no swags with us, but were all armed with
pick-axes and spades. Mr. Browning, who was of a
daring and impetuous nature, trusted solely to his pick
for his safety, while those behind had the advantage of
the footholds which we dug with our spades, each one
in turn widening the aperture, so that those in the rear
could ascend with comparative ease and safety. At the
request of Mr. Parks, our jolly old commander, I had
just finished yelling with tremendous vehemence a
verse of " The Englishman," which reverberated grandly

among the snowy peaks; Mr. Browning was in the act of scaling a steep and almost perpendicular ridge a few feet ahead of me; when, hearing a loud shout from the rear, " Hold on, Browning; for God's sake, hold on ;" I looked up just in time to avoid being swept away by Mr. Browning, who shot past me with terrible velocity, and travelled to the bottom of the pass in a few seconds. Nothwithstanding that he had passed within less than a foot of a jagged rock that jutted out in his road, and had spun round and round in his descent like a top, he experienced no further injury than a temporary numbness, a few severe scratches, and the total destruction of his apparel. After this, however, we foresaw that the difficulties of ascent on that side were too great to be surmounted, and it was decided by those upon whom the responsibility of our safety chiefly devolved that a fresh effort should be made entirely in a new direction.

Accordingly, on a bright, clear morning, the whole party, including those who had heen left behind on former occasions, together with Mr. Parks' party, set out from the wharry with swags packed with oatmeal, flour, sugar, and chocolate, each man's share being alike, and consisting of long narrow bags made to lie close within the blankets. After a heavy day's work we reached the summit; and, having taken a rest and a tot of grog all round from a bottle brought up on purpose, and which was thrown far and high over the cliff with three cheers, we six now set forward with our faces turned to Hokitika, prepared for roughing it in good earnest, whilst Mr. Parks and the rest of the party returned to the comfortable wharry which we had left far below.

After crossing a small lake and traversing a mile or so of ice valleys, we reached the head of a creek on the west side. The descent here was of a different nature to that on the east side of the range. After a gradual slope of some length, we came to a point beyond which there was no possible advance, except by a similar process to that which Mr. Browning had so involuntarily undergone before. This was to let ourselves go, and, trusting to the mercy of Providence, hope to glide safely to the bottom—the distance to be traversed before reaching a footing being, however, above a couple of hundred feet in this instance. After a hearty shake of the hand from all we were leaving, and another cheer, we one by one went down the incline as far as we could on our legs, and then throwing ourselves back shot down to the bottom without feeling anything beyond a slight shortening of the breath. And now came one of the most trying moments of my life. We were on the right hand slope of the range, and had to pass along its side about fifty feet above the edge of an abyss that fell sheer to the rocks below. The surface of the ice all along this part of the glacier was particularly hard and glassy, and every step we took had to be cut out. When Mr. Browning and I were about half way across we stopped for a moment and rested ; as the labour of chopping and cutting with a heavy spade, impeded by a bulky swag, was by no means trifling. The rest were some distance in the rear and evidently struggling on in our footsteps with no very lively feelings. Browning and I looked below us, looked ahead, and then at each other. " I'm half sorry we came this way now, Money," he said ; " but now we're here we must do our best ; it's not much further, at any rate." " I suppose we must," said I, " and the sooner the better." We waited till the others came up to us, and then screwed up our nerves, and slowly but surely accomplished the intervening distance. Mr. Browning had remembered this part of his journey in the summer, when the side along which he had crawled was covered with loose shingle from landslips far above ; but had avoided mention of its dangers, for fear of alarming us too soon, and what schoolboys call " establishing a funk." Once over this we had no great difficulty in rolling and scrambling to the bottom of the ravine, where lay yet before us huge rocks, cliffs, hills, and gullies covered with thick bush and deeply clothed with snow. We had seen no birds save a couple of ka-kas or parrots near the top of the saddle, who, though more than half frozen, managed to fly out of reach, and a disconsolate wood-hen, which disappeared in a snow-wreath.

Though rationed off for a short time to a pannikin of burgoo morning and evening, and half-a-dozen pieces of biscuit, we ran short by the time we arrived at a creek, beyond the regions of snow, which had been named Griffiths' Creek, after its finder. One of our party—our cook, an old sailor—had brought a dog with him which he assured us would catch wood-hens by the dozen, and when we had pitched camp at Griffiths' Creek, and were boiling our billy of burgoo for tea (being the only thing left in the way of food), the old chap strolled out to try for a chance of a duck, or anything he and his dog could get us. In less than half-an-hour he returned with three wood-hens and a pair of whistling ducks, which were soon plucked and popped into the pot.

A day or two of hard toil through thick bush and swamp brought us at last over a low saddle into the bed of the Styx river, the head waters of the Hokitika itself, at the mouth of which was the town of that name to which we were bound. Here we began to look out for signs of stores, which it had been arranged before our departure that we should find "planted" in the bush out of the reach of rats. After trudging some distance down the river-shed we at last came upon a pole stuck into a heap of large stones in a prominent position. To the top of it had been fastened a blade of flax, pointing into the bush on our right, where, after a short search, we discovered 100lbs. of flour, 50lbs. of sugar, tea, and oatmeal, besides a huge piece of bacon. This we soon attacked, and devoured panful after panful of fried bacon and damper, with copious libations of tea, before we threw ourselves on our beds of fern to smoke the postcœnal pipe with a sense of satiety and comfort which we had not experienced for some little time. We had expected to find also a couple of bottles of grog; but were disappointed in this, and were rather puzzled

as to the reason thereof. Whilst we were wondering
at the absence of the promised brandy, Mr. Browning
shouted from a little distance, " Smoke, by heaven ! "
We all started towards the direction in which he
pointed, and on reaching a piece of higher ground
could clearly see smoke a long distance away down the
river.

Mr. Browning immediately started in search of the
spot from which it emerged above the trees, and just as
we had finished the fifth or sixth frying-pan of bacon
and slapjacks, he returned with two men, and, better
still, with a bottle of Hollands, which was disposed of
with the utmost celerity and without a single wry face.
It appeared that a party had been sent up with the
stores to plant them in the bush, and to blaze a track
some distance up towards the low saddle in the direction
of Griffiths' Creek. After covering the things with
bundles of long grass made into the shape of half-
closed umbrellas, and hung from the boughs of trees,
the one who had charge of the party had arranged that
they should return on different sides of the river and
meet at the tent which they had pitched a few miles
down its bed. Accordingly they had started, the "boss"
taking with him one of the bottles of grog. and keeping one side of the stream, and his men taking the
other. He had never been since seen, and the men
who had come up with Mr. Browning had no idea
where he was. It was now two days since they had
parted ; he had been traced for some distance in the
bush, but his track was eventually lost sight of on the

H

edge of a steep bank overlooking a creek that ran into
the river. Both the creeks and the river itself had
been tremendously swollen by the heavy rain which
had fallen within the last few days, and they were
afraid that the poor fellow might have drank too freely
and been swept away by one of the torrents in attempting to ford it. We determined, according to Mr.
Browning's desire, to devote the next day to helping the
men in their endeavour to discover his fate ; and,
separating into different detachments, we followed up
every creek in the neighbourhood, searching without
success. Compelled at length, late in the evening, to
acknowledge that there was little hope of his being
alive, even if his body was not out at sea already, we
all turned our steps towards Hokitika, and in two days
arrived at a ferry opposite the township of Woodstock,
a few miles above Hokitika itself. Here we took a
storekeeper literally by storm, and cleared him out of
everything except a few boxes of sardines and half a
chest of tea. Another night saw us in Hokitika, our
hard-earned wages in our pockets, and free to go
whithersoever we pleased in search of fortune. It was
strange to me, having seen that coast when no other
white men but myself and my comrades previously
alluded to were on it, to enter a town like Hokitika,
with a splendid wharf, a court-house, post-office, police
camp, and nearly a hundred public-houses and hotels
already established.

A short spell, and away again across the sands to the
Grey River, from whence the reports had been of late

very attractive. The first thing I did was to look out
for work, and this I succeeded in obtaining the same
afternoon. The labour was similar in every respect to
that of a railway navvy. It consisted in the making
of a road cut along the sides of a low bush range on
the banks of the river Grey. The sides of these hills,
being in many places morasses, were continually sending down floods of yellow mud over the place where
we worked. The surveyor in charge of the work
was a thorough specimen of a gentleman, combined
with the character of a rough colonial bushman.
Though of very small stature, he was the fastest walker
through a heavy bush I ever came across. This I
found by experience when employed in cutting survey
lines with him a month or two subsequently. While
camped on the edge of the river, close to the scene
of our operations, we caught every day shoals of
white-bait ; a piece of gauze fastened to a circle of
supple-jack or bush cane, much resembling an ordinary
butterfly-net, was all that was required for their capture. Passing along the edge of the water, and drawing the net lightly and quickly below the surface, in
an hour's time one man would catch enough to fill
three or four large sized milk-pans. They are precisely
similar both in appearance and taste to those of the
Thames.

To describe the different peculiarities of character to
be met with amongst so strange an assortment from
all countries as the labourers on the bush-roads in the
colonies would require the pen of a Dickens. I have

found as much native wit and hearty appreciation of
humour among those who in the old country were
utterly rough and illiterate as among the polished and
refined members of the most civilized society. The
mind of the labouring man, dwarfed and stunted in its
development by the crushing sense of inferiority at
home, is enlarged and healthily braced by the freedom
and independence which so strikingly characterize a
colonial community.

One day, while filling my pipe, the ganger having
turned the corner of the bush the moment before, I
heard myself called, by tones familiar to my ear, and,
turning round, shook hands with my old friend, the
baker of the Six-mile. Surprised to see him carrying
his swag, knowing, as I did, that he had made a pile
out of that business, I asked him how things had been
going with him. He pulled out a fourpenny piece and
said, "That's my last coin, old man." Three or four
times in his New Zealand career he had made large
sums at his trade on the diggings, and lost all ; this
had been the case since I last saw him. He had in-
vested over a thousand pounds in some large dining-
rooms in Dunedin, and, though a steady man, with a
hard-working wife and children, had ultimately entirely
failed. He was now on his way up to the Grey, with
the intention of building an oven on the first rush he
should come to, and of once more making a fair start.
Having already overdrawn my week's wages, I regretted being unable to help him with a note ; but as he
was well-known on the diggings, I had little doubt of

his getting on as well as he could wish. A few weeks completed the part of the road for which Dobson had contracted ; and on his asking me to join him in working a boat on Lake Brunner, I immediately agreed, and we pulled together very well. He was now engaged in making a survey line for the road, to follow round the northern corner of the lake in the direction of the Teremakau. This would eventually form the high road between Christchurch and the township on the Grey River. My work in the boat was the conveyance of the necessary stores for those of the hands, including myself, who were living with him in tents at the furthest extremity of the projected line. Meantime the contract for the making of the road itself had been undertaken by two men, under whom I engaged myself on leaving Dobson. I was compelled to work considerably harder for these gentlemen, as the wages given by private contractors are in proportion to the amount of work done. But as long before this I had acquired considerable dexterity in the use of the axe, I managed to give satisfaction, and remained on the work until it was finished.

There being nothing further to do in this quarter, I left the lake for the Arnold township, a mile or two from the banks of the Grey. Here I resumed my old trade of packing, and found plenty to keep me in constant employment. Engaged in the same occupation was a Frenchman who had been noted for carrying enormous weights up the most difficult ascents in the South Island. He was in the habit of trudging

"through bush, through briar," under the burden of
two cwt., with as much ease as a man would in ordinary
cases under a knapsack of a few lbs. weight. When
it is considered that 25s. per cwt. was given for every
four miles, and that we could perform that distance
(including the back journey) twice every day, my
readers will hardly wonder at our continuing in so
lucrative a line of business, although the ground
traversed was of such a nature as to make the labour
treble what it would have been on any ordinary road.
My average earnings were from £2 to £2 10s. per day.
For some time we monopolised the market as before on
the Six-mile. The game, however, was too good to last;
as the supply of labour increased, the profit decreased
in proportion, and I was again about to travel when an
old mate arrived in the township from Lake Brunner. He
brought the news that some men, of whom I had heard
for some time past, had gone down to the Warden at
Greymouth to take out a prospecting claim on a river
at the further side of the lake. Having been in their
confidence, he knew the direction in which they had
made the discovery which had induced them to take
this step. We delayed no longer than was required to
get a few necessaries together, and with 50 lbs. of
flour and our blankets were on the road next morning.
The diggers who were supposed to have made this find
were distinguished by rather peculiar pseudonyms.
The one was called " Warregal," which is, I believe, the
name of an animal in Australia; while the other was
known to his friends and the public as " Kangaroo

Jem." Although among the first to reach the shores of the lake were those of our little party, *i. e.*, Fraser, who had brought me the news, and a few others who smelt a rat, yet the evening of the following day saw nearly 2000 men encamped on the edge of its waters, and the scene previously described on the Six-mile was here re-enacted, and on the very spot where poor Howitt and his companions had met with so melancholy an ending to their enterprise. I found that the contractors for whom I had been working had anticipated, if not organised, the rush, and had prepared for it by building a large boat for the passage over the lake of the ex-pectant diggers, and a large store for the sale of pro-visions and grog for their support. Notwithstanding the good appearance that the whole affair bore on its surface, I determined to be careful how I followed what might turn out to be a mere "Will-o'-the-wisp," and I obtained places at the oars for myself and mate at the rate of £1 per trip across the lake. The boat was a sort of large whale-boat, drawing about two feet of water; it carried from forty to fifty diggers with their swags, besides the crew. Day and night, as the numbers increased, were we compelled to work; and, as fifteen shillings was the price of the fare across for every man, the prospects of the owners seemed bright indeed. After quite three thousand men had been taken over to the neighbourhood of the "rush," the run on the boat became rather less overpowering, and a feeling pre-vailed that news would be very acceptable from the scene of operations.

One fine morning (I had at this time left the boat for a day's spell) we were surprised to see the boat coming over nearly full, and that instead of coming straight to land they held off shore, resting on their oars some hundred yards from us. The owners shouted to know what they intended to do with the boat, and the answer came pealing most irascibly over the water towards us, " Give up the prospectors, or we will burn and sink your boat." I knew where the prospectors were, but not knowing the rights of the case I considered it none of my business.

The owners meantime denied all knowledge of their whereabouts, and refused, if they did know, to tell their "location." The men in the boat now turned the coxswain of the boat into the water, which at that part was over his middle, and he was compelled to wade ashore as best he could. They waited some time, apparently in doubt what to do next, and then pulled quietly back to whence they had come. From that time complete possession was taken of the boat, and all who had previously gone over the lake with high hopes of making their piles were brought back with feelings of deep indignation against their deceivers. I have never felt sure to this day whether the contractors, both of whom I knew and had found good pay-masters and straightforward in their dealings, really were or were not culpably concerned in the affair; but the whole thing certainly looked like it.

It seems that on arriving at the opposite side of the lake those poor deluded people had found a frightful country of tangled bush, swamp, and river, so bad as to compel many of them to throw their provisions and even blankets and tents away on the road ; and after many hours and, in some cases days, of hard travelling and every kind of privation and exposure, had only arrived to find the whole thing what is called in digging parlance a " duffer "—*i. e.*, that there was comparatively "nothing" to repay them for even the trouble of digging a single hole.

After the greater part had been brought over and were once more camped on the edges of the lake, grog-tents began to spring up on all sides, and the excitement amongst the disappointed crowds became intense, and so exasperated were they against the prospectors that if they had been discovered at that time they would have been torn limb from limb. They, however, managed to keep close enough. Although I myself knew where they were located, there were not half-a-dozen who did.

Meantime I continued to work for the contractors, and got good pay for even an hour's work, while the other unfortunates were compelled to spend the little they possessed or to borrow enough provisions to last them for a time. One afternoon, when there had been a good deal of drinking going on throughout the canvas village, I noticed a look about the Irish who were collected around the store that I was sure portended some outbreak. I went over to the store to see Potter, one of the contractors whom I mentioned as having built the boat and supplied the provisions. I found him lying on a bundle of fern at the back part of the store, and pushed through the crowd to shake hands with him. He looked queer, I thought, and kept one hand in the breast of his blue shirt while he spoke to me. "Get me a stiff glass of rum, Money," said he; "mine's all drunk an hour ago." He tossed it off, and I had just got, glass in hand, a few yards back towards the grog-tent, when I heard a shout, and, looking round, saw the mob pouring out of Potter's store laden with every description of "tucker." Knowing that I could do nothing to prevent the row, I went with the crowd to look on. It was an extraordinary sight. There was a bearded giant shouldering a couple of sides of bacon; here a smaller but equally hairy "Knight of the pick" staggering under the load of 100 lbs. of flour and a handkerchief full of tobacco, there a Yankee "sliding" with a chest of tea, while a small and select company were sharing the contents of a huge grass-bag of sugar. In all directions were seen lucky marauders laden with hams, rolls of spiced beef or bacon, tins of coffee, and tools, tin dishes, and the other contents of a store supplied with the requisites for a "digging establishment." Ten minutes' hard work cleared the place, and another ten saw the canvas torn down for tents, &c., and the rafters, wall-plates, and fern-tree sides knocked down for fire-wood. A strange instance of irresolution was seen during the scrimmage. A man who was taking a "nip" five minutes before in the shanty that I had entered for the rum, and whom I had noticed as having a gun in his hand, went quietly to the beach where the large boat belonging to Potter's store was lying, and, unfastening the "painter," walked backwards into the lake, holding the rope in his hand, and pushing the boat along with him. When the water had nearly reached his waist he stopped, and, raising the gun, swore he would shoot any man who came to take the boat from him. For a moment all around seemed taken aback by the man's attitude and apparent determination, when suddenly a tall Irishman, marching straight into the water, and wading up to him, wrenched the gun out of his hands, broke it over the gunwale of the boat, and threw the pieces far into the waters of the lake. The wretched braggart shrunk away just in time to save himself from a similar punishment to that I once saw bestowed on a pickpocket at the Six-mile. It occurred on the morning of one of the first Sundays after the rush had set in. There were three fights going on at the same time and a tremendous crush in the street, when I heard a shout of "Thief, thief," followed by yells of " Lynch the beggar !" " String him up !" &c., &c. I climbed up on the highest point near me, and there I saw the poor wretch dragged by a hundred hands in the direction of a saw-pit behind the township. It was a toss-up for his life ; but he was let off eventually with a fearful "hiding," and an injunction never to show his face again on those " diggings."

CHAPTER IX.

THE rush on Lake Brunner being now at an end, I set off for Hokitika, selling my bag of flour on the way at half its value. In Hokitika I got work directly from the same gentleman who had asked me to join his party over the ranges in the winter. He had the contract to make a clear track through the bush, half-a-chain wide, on the Kanieri River, which runs into the Hokitika a few miles up. Though 12s. a-day was not much then, and particularly for ten hours' work, it was better than nothing, so I shouldered an axe, and taking as mate a young fellow whom I had known in Canterbury, I turned to. The work was light enough, though the ganger was a nigger-driver of the worst type, who fancied that no man who spoke the Queen's English could do a day's work (a very common idea in the colonies, and, I am sorry to say, in many instances only too true). He was consequently discontented with the work I did. This did not fret me much, as I knew what I was worth ; but what did fret me and my companion were the mosquitoes. The track went along the banks of the Kanieri River, and these, being overflowed in every fresh with the muddy waters from marsh lands above, were coated with a layer of white slime, which, when the river went down, dried to a fine dust. This bred and harboured clouds of mosquitoes, and not only all night were we tortured by millions of them in the tent, but all day, from dawn to sunset, every shrub we removed, and every fern and sapling we cleared away, sent out a fresh army to harass us. In vain we surrounded our heads with fern-branches and grass, or tied handkerchiefs round our chins ; nose, eyes, ears, and mouth were at the same moment invaded, while every few seconds the bare hands and arms had to be rubbed clear of the bloodthirsty little demons. It sometimes became almost too much to endure, and more than once or twice I have hurled my tools into the bush and swore that I would give it up. I do not think that I slept more than one hour every night during those five weeks on the Kanieri. Half-a-dozen times during the night would we rise and sit at the fire, smoking and talking. We tried every device in turn, from burning cow and horse dung, brought from the township, to rubbing ourselves with oil. Nothing kept them off; the oil repelled them whilst it was wet, but as soon as it became dry it was useless. That short quarter of an hour during which the wretches could do nothing was a season of heavenly rest.

Six weeks or so finished the clearing as far as Mr. Griffiths had contracted for, and once more I turned my steps towards the Grey River. On the way I stopped a night at the Teremakau, and, hearing that hands were wanted for canoeing up the river, I enlisted at once. After a trip or two I managed well enough, and found my old Buller experience of great use to me in handling the pole or the paddle. We had to load the canoe with cases of spirits, tubs of butter, chests of tea, and bags of flour, besides boxes of candles and packages of salt, sugar, tobacco, &c. From 15 cwt. to a ton was our usual loading, and when we came to rapids or falls we had to wade up them against a tremendous current, tugging at the end of a long trail-rope, till we literally pulled the canoe with its freight up the fall, and into deep water again. We did ten miles up the river every day, starting at nine o'clock, and getting up to the creek, where we delivered the goods about two. Here, after a sufficient rest, we jumped in again, and singing and shouting to the echoing woods on every side of us, we flew down the river at a glorious pace, with appetites like horses, and ready fully to enjoy the warm fire and good feed that awaited us.

For this work I got £1 5s. for each trip, and as I returned to the comforts of the township every night it was a great improvement on the Kanieri road and its mosquitoes, its ten hours' work, and half the pay. As this, however, like many other things in this world was too good to last, I returned to Hokitika, and from there, accompanied by a friend named Jackson (ex-lieutenant of 2nd Rifles), made some miles on my way to Christchurch. Here, at a shanty at the foot of the Arahura, Jackson and I, over a parting glass, pledged each other in the most virtuous resolutions, to "eschew sack," and begin to live soberly. I never saw him after that night; but a jolly little saddler, who came home in the same ship with me in June, 1868, told me that Jackson had, most unfortunately for himself, had some money left him, and that he was, when last heard of, flying round (as Jemmy expressed it) like a paper man in a gale of wind.

A few days' hard walking saw me in Christchurch, and from thence, determining to give the diggings, at least for a time, the cut direct, I took my passage in the "Wellington," New Zealand Navigation Co.'s steamer, for Wellington, where I arrived safe, and, putting up at the best hotel, began to look about me.

Lieutenant-colonel McDonnell was staying there at this time, and with him, after a few days in Wellington, I went down to Wanganui. The name of this gallant officer has been so repeatedly before the public that it is scarcely necessary to add my mite of praise to the deserved *kudos* (κὐδος) which he has gained for himself, but if the opinion of one who served (however unworthily) under his command, and has been close to him in moments of danger and difficulty, is of the smallest value, I may here assert my conviction that not only has the colonial army never had a braver or more energetic and determined officer, but that, with the single exception of the brave and lamented Von Tempsky, no individual man has done more to bring the Maori war to a decisive issue. If he had not been restrained and hampered by the "penny wise and pound foolish" system which some miserable carpet-knights have fostered and encouraged, the news of the fatal affair at Te-nhatu-te-mana, when poor Von Tempsky met his premature end, would never have been told.

In the steamer "Wanganui" we embarked for the port of that name on the West Coast, and, after a few weeks spent there at the only really comfortable hotel in the place, called the "Wanganui," and kept by a fine old soldier, I began to think of a move. I had enjoyed my "spell" very much, and had been delighted at meeting an old chum in the 14th, one of the jolliest, best-hearted fellows I ever knew. Between his mess-room and the acquaintance of one or two Christchurch friends, I managed to while away a month very pleasantly, but saw no more hope of employment than I had done in Wellington. McDonnell, however, had not forgotten me, and I determined to go up and work on the survey till there was a vacancy in the Wanganui Yeomanry Cavalry, which I wished to enter. Accordingly, I left town on the same day that the Maori contingent or friendly natives (who had taken service under the command of Colonel McDonnell's brother) started on their way to the front. Captain Newland, of the Patea Rangers, very kindly asked me to share the tent in which Captain McDonnell (the officer in command), with himself and one or two others, located themselves while on the march. The arrangements were quite different to anything in the service, but both Captain McDonnell and Lieutenant Gudgeon were extremely kind and hospitable.

Arrived at Patea, the head quarters, I lunched with a Mr. B———, who afterwards had the command of the Wanganui Yeomanry Cavaly, and walked over the same afternoon to Kakaramea, where a body of militia were stationed, and also some surveyors. Here I applied to Mr. P. Smith, at his tent, as I had heard that he required hands, and I had brought a letter of introduction which Mr. Carrington, chief surveyor, had been kind enough to write for me. Mr. Smith at once asked me to put up with him until he had a vacancy, which would be in a day or two. I accepted this offer, and, one of the party leaving shortly after for Taranaki, I took his place in the men's tents and turned to with a will. This sort of work is pretty rough sometimes, though comparatively nothing to one who had scrambled with a heavy swag through the wilds of the West Coast. The line of survey has to be taken across a certain country and through it ; though it should be full of precipices, torrents, or thick tangled and heavy bush and undergrowth, the party with their bill-hooks and fern slashers must cut their way. The wear and tear of clothes is ruinous ; the strongest leather would hardly stand the thick, rough fern, the perpetual friction of the barks of fallen trees, and the constant contact with scrub and briar of every description ; and, being a kind of work that goes on in nearly all weathers, it happens that sometimes, for days together, unless he carry with him a wardrobe more extensive than mine ever was, a man is liable to be wet through from morning till night. I was beginning to get into the ways of the party (for no two employers that I ever worked under in the bush conducted their operations exactly alike), when, just as we had moved farther up towards the front, the farrier of the troop in which I was awaiting the first vacancy took his discharge, and I stepped into his place. I was sworn in

I

as trooper to serve for the remainder of the three years
(some eighteen months of which had already elapsed),
for which period the Wanganui Yeomanry Cavalry
were engaged.

In the same tent with me was more than one whom
I had known before : Tom Holland, who had once
owned a large station in Canterbury, and whom I had
known when flashing about in Auckland ; and poor
Pat Hanley, an old chum in the Auckland force, afterwards shot at my side in a night attack on the village
of Kitionetea. They were a jolly crowd, that rowdy,
reckless, generous, hardy, headlong old troop, and I
often feel thankful for the year I spent with them ; for
the experience gained by association with men of every
stamp brought into hourly collision, and shewing, as
they must do in like positions, every strong point of
character, has made me think better of human nature.
Two days after I joined I was out with some dozen or
so as an escort to Colonel McDonnell, who wished to
reconnoitre the neighbourhood of the Ketemerai bush,
which both then and afterwards was a nest of Hau-
haus. We were riding along in threes, about two
hundred yards from the bush, when we heard a couple
of shots, evidently signals. The word was given immediately, "Trot," and we removed to a respectable
distance, where we should at least not be such easy pots
for the concealed niggers. From the place where we
halted, about 600 yards' distance from the bush, we saw
the niggers come outside, and some mounted men riding
to and fro.

Presently a body advanced with a white flag, upon which Colonel McDonnell and his orderly, with one or two others, galloped towards them. They had a corero or parley for some time, while we tightened our girths and looked to our carbines in case of a row. Presently Tom Holland, who was the colonel's orderly, came back, singing out for a box of matches for the Maories. I was foolish enough to give a box I had brought in my pocket, not knowing the use to which we afterwards found they turned them, and he rode back with them to Colonel McDonnell, who was still talking to the Maories. Suddenly there seemed to be a movement among them, and back came Colonel McDonnell and his little party, while the white flag retreated rapidly to the bush again. Not a second after the Colonel and party had pulled up in front of us came a volley right over our heads. We immediately advanced nearer, and a few shots were fired; but the natives had entered the bush, where it was useless to follow them, and we contented ourselves with driving home a small mob of cattle which had been surrounded by one or two under the direction of our farrier-major, Duff, the most energetic and plucky little fellow in the whole force.

Hostilities having been thus declared, the order came out the same day that an expedition would start on a certain evening, and that every man was to carry two days' provisions in his haversack. We were to take and destroy the village of Pokaikai at dawn the next morning, a time when Maories were more particularly inclined to sleep. Those of the Wanganui troop who chose to do so were permitted to volunteer on foot, a certain number only being sent mounted, to remain at the approaches to the village, and in readiness for action at a moment's notice. I had not had a horse "told off" to me at this time, consequently I volunteered on foot for the expedition. We halted several times during the night, and those who could snatched a short sleep in the high fern. Before daylight in the morning we were close to the village of Pokaikai. Here the word was passed for dead silence, and we approached with cautious steps, listening to the occasional crowing of cocks, or a dog's bark, in the bush close ahead of us. When within a hundred yards we lay down for the last time before the final rush in the fern, beside the narrow foot-track by which we had come, awaiting the word to advance. All the rest of the affair was a sudden up-rising of ghostly figures, a stealthy creeping along the narrow track ; then the word "Charge !" and a mad, shouting, leaping host of dark forms bounding down the side of a gully, across a creek, and up the other side, where a scene followed much like fireworks on the fifth of November, except that the explosions were from deadly barrels instead of the harmless squibs and crackers of our childish recollections. The village was sacked, and the "wharries" one after another set fire to and burnt, and then "Home" was the word. Once out of the bush, we were allowed to make the best of our way back, which we did in groups of two or three at a time, nor were any of us sorry to reach camp and have a feed and a roll in the blankets. A few days subsequently the Hau-haus made a raid on our troop-horses, and drove them off in the night into the bush. This was only to be expected from the careless provision made for their safety by Mr. B———, who commanded us. After evening stables they were turned out into a flat below the hill where we were encamped, and allowed to remain there till morning, with no guard over them and no fence to prevent them from wandering. The most natural consequence of such carelessness was what actually occurred. We made another expedition to a village called Mere-mere, where we discovered most of the horses amongst the clearings. My poor brute had fallen down a potato pit when we found him, and was dead. Poor 95! (our horses were all branded with a number) I fear I rejoiced at thy sad misfortune, as thy bones were over old for service, and I soon after obtained a better animal than thee.

Shortly after, we moved up to a further position than we had yet occupied, called, in consequence of a small patch of low timber, " The Round Bush." Here we formed regular " lines " for our horses with a stout rope stretched along posts firmly sunk in the ground, and the horses, after being " tailed," or shepherded, all day by one of us "told off" for that purpose, were tied in rows on each side of the rope for the night, and were bedded down with fern. Here I was on escort duty for some time, accompanying a dray with provisions to a position still further in advance, where Colonel McDonnell was now building a strong redoubt called Ketemerai. As an escort we were worse than useless, for we were never more than three men with a corporal or sergeant in charge, and this number, without being enough to repel any attack, was sufficient to tempt the Maories to attack us and plunder the dray, which indeed soon afterwards happened.

One morning, after having been with two others on this duty for nearly a fortnight, I was sent on fatigue duty instead, and a man named Haggerty, formerly a soldier in the 40th, took my place on the escort. It was noticed that, though, like all old soldiers, a particularly tidy man in his dress at all times, his turn-out that morning was unusually correct. His boots shone like glass, his breeches were new and fitted like a glove, and his saddlery and accoutrements were faultlessly clean. An ambush was laid by the Maories behind some flax bushes, a little distance from the track by which the escort had to pass, and when only a few hundred yards frem the bush, some forty Maories fired a volley at them, and poor Haggerty fell. The rest behaved very well, retiring in the most orderly manner, and guarding the driver of the dray and a militia man who accompanied it until relief came from the redoubt, which was only about half a mile distant, and from which the whole affair had been seen distinctly. Meantime, some of the cowardly wretches surrounded poor Haggerty, whose horse had been shot, and who had fallen with his leg beneath it in such a position that he was unable to draw his revolver, and finished him with their tomahawks. When the relief from the redoubt came up to him, they found him with his sheath-knife drawn in his hand, and his face hacked in the most horrible mannner by the Maories' tomahawks.

There was a strong feeling on the part of every man in the troop that poor Haggerty should not be unavenged, and more than one tattooed villain paid the penalty for the dastardly murder of our poor comrade. If it had not been for the miserable inefficiency of the old shopkeeper who held the command of our gallant little body (the members of which had won fame under their formerly deservedly popular officer, Captain Percy, and who still boasted of as brave a little cornet as ever wore a silver-laced forage cap), the strong *esprit de corps* that existed amongst us would have rendered all our *désagrémens* trifling. Mr. B———, having been a drill sergeant at a cavalry depôt at home some quarter of a century before, was supposed to be just the man for the command of a rough and ready troop, composed of every class of adventurer, and fighting against a savage race like the Maories in the wilds of New Zealand. He was extremely unpopular, from the utter unsuitableness of his age and habits, and, more especially, from his absurd pedantry in matters of drill, dress, etc. Strictness in these matters may be necessary enough in a showy body of men, such as mounted police or a crack regiment in Her Majesty's service, but is not to be compared in point of real use to the active, hardy habits of a New Zealand bushman, and the rough and ready energy and endurance that will go through any hardships, and stand against any odds. When to these disadvantages there was added a personal vulgarity of manner and offensiveness of address that were both disgusting and exasperating, it will not be a matter of surprise that men who had been accustomed to be commanded by gentlemen, and themselves to be treated as such, should at length, on his attempting a gross injustice to their whole body, rebel against him and refuse to fight any longer under so unworthy a leader. But I anticipate.

CHAPTER X.

WILL not attempt to go through a history of the campaign under Colonel McDonnell, as it would only prove wearisome ; and with the account of the only engagement of any consequence in which I took part will end this portion of my adventures.

Right in front of us, under the shade of Mount Egmont and far in the bush, we could see the smoke daily from a large village called Pungarahu, said to be a nest of Hau-haus. This McDonnell determined to destroy in the same manner as we had done all that we had yet come across, viz. : to shoot down all who resisted, and burn it to the ground. Accordingly, one night the whole force mustered in dead silence, armed with rifles and carbines, and each man carrying as many rounds as he could beyond his regular number in a haversack behind him. Altogether, I believe we numbered about 180 strong, including the friendly Maories or native contingent, who always accompanied us, but who, with scarcely an exception, were looked upon by us as worse than useless.

We proceeded as usual, marching in single file, down to the beach, to a place called Wangangoro, where a company of the 18th Royal Irish were quartered. Here we had to cross by means of a canoe, which had been thrown across the wide and deep gorge of a rapid and rocky river which ran into the sea at this place. A poor fellow, who had once held a commission in the rifles, and who was a private in the militia at this time, fell over a boulder in descending the precipitous ravine, and broke his arm. He was taken up to the hospital of the 18th in the redoubt, and, being to some extent deprived of the use of his arm, afterwards received a pension of 1s. per diem for his life. After marching as usual all night, we reached the village of Pangarahu just before dawn the next morning, and jumped over the fences with a rush.

The " wharries " were perfectly full of rebels, some of whom we shot down as they ran for their lives to the bush, whilst others remained inside and fired out on us from their low door-ways. Our little farrier-major, Duff, with customary Irish impetuosity, was as usual one of the first in the place, and I caught sight of him firing off all the barrels of his revolver in reckless style round the corner of a "wharry" door into the inside, which was crammed with niggers. The next minute I was potting an old villain with a head like an oakum mop in dry weather, and he had just dropped when I heard some one shout "Duff's down !" I instantly ran towards the spot where I had seen him last ; the Hau-haus had been cleared out of the hut, and on the ground beside it sat poor Duff shot through the neck. With the help of the troop sergeant-major of the Wellington Defence Force, I carried him off to the doctor, and left him to his care, though it was but too evident that all was over with him. Five minutes after this, Colonel McDonnell himself and Captain Newland shouted for volunteers to follow them and clear the " wharries " and bush at the further end of the village, from which a dropping fire had begun. We had not gone half way across the open towards the bush before a sudden and heavy fire opened from the trees above us, and looking round I found that besides Colonel McDonnell and Captain Newland, there was not half-a-dozen of us to do any good. Colonel McDonnell saw this, and gave the word to take cover. After a skedaddle across the open, I dropped under a fence, from which several of us kept up a fire for some time. Whilst firing and loading under this frail protection, a poor fellow who had volunteered on this expedition was hit out in the open in front of us, and I had to pass over the " tie-up," and give a hand to carry him in. He was a high-spirited, brave fellow, and was in the act of bringing a wounded Maori prisoner out of the line of fire when he was knocked over ; he died before we got home. The fire which had so unexpectedly broken out from the trees was known afterwards to have been from a large reinforcement of the rebels, who had arrived suddenly from a large village some way in the interior of the bush, and which we afterwards, in company with some of the 18th, and honoured by the presence of Sir George Grey himself, took and burned down. By this time we had several wounded, and as each man required four to carry his stretcher, besides relays, our numbers had dwindled considerably ; the Maories never for a moment thinking of helping to carry their " Pakeha "

comrades, dead or wounded. The numbers of the
enemy seemed to be momentarily increasing, and the
word was passed to take the wounded out of the place
as quickly as possible, the rest retiring as steadily as
might be in their rear. When this movement began,
I and some half-dozen others were formed into a rear
guard, under the command of one of the coolest and
most fearless fellows it has ever been my lot to come
across, Ensign Northcroft, of the Taranaki Military
Settlers. He had lost his cap, and, with a handkerchief tied round his head, took charge of our little party,
with the injunction, "Keep low down, and fire away
boys!" ' I obeyed the first part of this order after a
time only too willingly, for as sounds from the main
body, who were in full retreat, became less and less
distinct, the shouts and yells from the Hau-haus from
all sides became perfectly fiendish, and the balls began
to rattle about the trees above us in anything but a
pleasing manner. I lay on the ground, half way down
the slope of a small gully just below the village, flat on
my stomach, potting at hazard, with my carbine in
front of me, in the direction of the loudest cries and
at the puffs of smoke from the rebels in their leafy
ambush. For a short time I candidly acknowledge
that I was not entirely free from the sensation known
by schoolboys as blue funk ; and when my readers remember that we were being rapidly hemmed in, and by
so blood-thirsty a set of brutes as the Ngatirannuis
have proved themselves to be, yelling, shrieking, and
closing fast upon our little band, whilst the leaves and

twigs falling about us shewed the extent of ammunition they were bestowing on the hated "Pakeha," and that we were aware that the main body were by this time out of hearing, perhaps they will excuse the sinking sensation of one heart in that row of bodies, crouched like deer-stalkers within sight of their game.

All at once a voice reached us—"Mr. Northcroft, you can retire slowly." "Steady, boys, up into the bush; quick with you." To snatch up carbine, and, bending low, to scud like a hare up the opposite slope and into the bush, has taken as long a time to write as I employed to accomplish it; but, once beyond their friendly shade, we soon, though keeping up our fire as we went, and moving steadily, reached the rear of the main body, and all were shortly afterwards halted on a clearing, where we turned to to make stretchers out of blankets (one of which each man had brought with him) for the better conveyance of the wounded men, three of whom died before we reached the redoubt we had left in the morning.

Taking turn about at the duty of shouldering the stretchers, we reached the Wangangaro Redoubt early in the afternoon, and were served out with a "doubler," or two lots of grog in one.

I took a last look at the poor fellows lying in a row sewn up in their blankets, who had started the night before, "burning with high hope," and so soon "to moulder cold and low," and was not sorry to turn in early that night, pretty well baked. We had a few more expeditions after this, and it was while advancing with the 18th to take the village of Kitionitea, that we were surprised by an out picket, who had felled huge trees across the track and built their mia-mias behind them, and poor Pat Hanley, my old comrade in Auckland, was killed.

I could tell many curious incidents peculiar to this sort of life if I did not fear that they would prove tame and uninteresting from so unskilled a pen, so I will not enter further upon this part of my erratic experiences, only mentioning that what had been long brewing in our wild band soon came to a head.

Mr. B——— actually went so far, on our gallant and popular sergeant-major leaving us to join his brother (a major in a regiment at the Cape, I believe), as to appoint in his place, over the heads of all our own non-commissioned officers who had been with the troop over two years and through its hardest days, a private trooper from the Wellington Defence Force. He was a steady man and a good rider, but had nothing further to recommend him (beyond the fact of his being a popular and intelligent fellow) to a position above the heads of many equally qualified, and whose claims, not only from the superior rank to which they had risen in the troop, but from the mere fact of their belonging to the old Wanganui Yeomanry Cavalry, gave them a right of precedence for promotion. We were electrified one evening, whilst attending the sale by auction of the property of one of our deceased comrades, by reading in the order-book the appointment of Trooper O'Halloran, of the Wellington Defence

Force, to be sergeant-major of the Wanganui Yeomanry Cavalry, in the place of Sergeant-major Hall, retired· Every man instantly refused to do further duty as long as this order was carried out. The whole of us, therefore, were put under arrest, and after a pleasant enough month, during which we drew our rations and had plenty of exercise and recreation, were one by one tried by a court-martial, and one and all honourably acquitted. Mr. B——— shortly afterwards gave up his command.

The country having now become moderately quiet, Colonel McDonnell, if he had been allowed to carry out the measures he desired, would probably have secured permanent safety to the settlers and merchants who began to occupy the district ; but, as has always been the case where the right man was for once in the right place, the penny-wise Government could not see it as those did who had followed the course of events in the district, and, acted upon by the representations of interested office-seekers, actually had the face to break their agreement with the men of the militia force, who had been sworn in for three years at a fixed rate of pay. They sent up Colonel G———, who had been known to say to men discharged from the service that he hoped they would starve in the streets, and who had suggested the expediency of the measure to re-enrol these very men, before the time for which they had agreed to serve had expired, at a rate of little more than half the amount of wages they had engaged for. In case of their not accepting this offer, they were to be

shewn the land that was to be theirs when their time
was up, and to be allowed to settle on it, or get their
living as well as they could.

The greater part of the troop left the service at once,
disgusted with such treatment at the instance of a mad-
brained official whose sole recommendation for promotion in the colonial army consisted in his having commanded a company in the regulars in so ridiculous a
manner as to render his retirement, if not necessary, at
least advantageous to his regiment; and yet this miserable humbug had the power of harassing and hindering
McDonnell's measures in every possible way. The re-
sult has been chiefly owing to that worthy's clever
manœuvre to save a penny for government, with the
benevolent intention of spending a pound eventually.
The accounts which reached me after my return to
England did not in the least degree astonish me. I
only regretted that he who had been one of the main
causes of the bloodshed at Turo-turo-mokai—the blood,
too, of men like Ross and others, who had shewn their
pluck and gallantry in many a wild encounter with
their savage foes—should not have been the first victim
to his own folly, and that thus any future errors of
such magnitude might be prevented.

I took work on the survey again, and that not proving steady enough, I began to cut firewood in the bush
and sell it in the town. With three good fellows in
an old "wharry" in the Kakaramea Redoubt, I carried
this on for about a month, till that also became an un-
certain employment, and I joined an old troop-mate

who had been post-and-rail splitting for some Maories
at Rangitiki, to which place I went with him.   I
worked for some time for a Maori chief, who actually
lived in a boarded house and kept an English cook.
It was amusing enough to see the crowd of dirty beggars, some with nothing but a filthy blanket to cover
their bodies, while others were rigged in paper collars
and bobtail coats and jewellery, sitting around the
deal table in the kitchen, stuffing hot mashed potatoes
and lumps of fat pork into their mouths with both
hands, and believing all the time that they were be-
having in the most correct way, and were, in fact,
almost adepts in civilization.   The old chief, Reuben,
looked upon himself as a sort of Marquis of Hastings,
after he had imbibed too much bad rum, and had lost
two or three shillings, not pounds, at a sitting.   He
used to set off every evening on a broken-down hack,
with an Inverness cape over him, to play "loo" in the
most reckless manner for penny points !

I found some difficulty in getting even my week's
wages out of the dirty old tattooed savage ; but, by
some blarney and more bounce, I succeeded in doing
what scarcely any had done before, and vowed that it
should be my last experiment in that line.

I next took a job at splitting posts and rails on a
station close by the Maories, which promised to pay
me fairly enough.   It is pleasant, clean work, and the
healthiest a man can do, though pretty hard and requiring considerable strength as well as knowledge of
the use of the axe.   This employed me for about six

J

weeks, during which time we had a small place to live in, that to our ideas, accustomed to tent-life, was a little palace. It had been used as a wash-house, and the fire-place was famously big. Besides this, we revenged ourselves on the Maories, whose pah was on the other side of the creek near us, by lying in wait for their pigs as they came across the stream, and slaughtering them for our table whenever we happened to be out of meat.

This job finished, I set off down the coast in the direction of Manawatu, and took work on a large farm at Rangitiki. Mr. McBeth was the only Swedenborgian I ever came across, and a most kind-hearted, exemplary character he was in every way. His house was like a home, and I look back to my life there as to a pleasant dream. I took the job of hedge-trimming at first, and, after having finished this all round the station land, which consisted of some 1500 acres parcelled off into paddocks and fields, I began to pick up bullock-driving ; and many a day I have awoke in the morning with stiff limbs from walking over the heavy ploughed land all day behind my bullocks, while they dragged the iron harrow after them, whilst I constantly shouted at them, every now and then lifting the heavy frame of the harrow to free it from roots and weeds collected by it in its progress. Dagging and paring sheep, tailing lambs, etc., felling timber, and splitting firewood, were the other employments in which I spent three months at Mr. McBeth's farm very pleasantly. A reduction of expenses, and consequently of farm hands, caused me to leave this worthy gentleman sooner than I would have wished, and I entered the employment of a neighbouring settler, who remembered me years before when I was digging on the Lammerlaw Creek, in Otago, where he kept the store from which we obtained our provisions. Here I had to work on an average fourteen hours a-day to satisfy Mr. Brice, who was a Scotchman, and tried to make ninepence go as far as other people's shilling. Being the only hand kept, my duties were more arduous still, and I rather astonished my employer by packing his wool, on my first trial, closer than he had ever had it done before. What I liked about this place was that the hours of the morning and evening were devoted entirely to dairy work, such as churning, filling the dishes with fresh milk, etc.; though, of course, feeding the calves, pigs, ducks, etc., formed part of the programme of the entertainment. The amount of milk and cream I consumed while in this farm I should be sorry to attempt to calculate. Mr. Brice's sister not being blessed with angelic sweetness of temper, and having abused me one day about some trifle, I next day went in search of "fresh fields and pastures new." Before three days I obtained a contract for the erection of a scrub fence, and, having hunted up a mate, who was a hard-working chap, "wired into" the work, and in less than two months had cleared a sum that gave us £30 for the time we had been at it; this in a farming district, where wages were nearly as low as at home, was not very bad, especially as I had never put up a fence of the kind before.

Tired of farm life, I took a run up to Patea to see
how things looked up there, and, after finding nothing
doing that would pay, joined the colonial army for
the third time, and drew my rations and lived in a
bell-tent for a month, at the end of which time we
were disbanded, and I began to think seriously of turning again towards the diggings, when a letter reached
me with the intelligence that the dearest friend I had
on earth wished me to come home immediately. This
decided me on giving up my wanderings at least for a
time, and in less than three weeks I found myself
steaming out of Wellington harbour in the Panama
Company's ship "Kaikaura," bound for *Home* after
just seven years' absence.

We had pretty rough weather to Panama, but the
"Kaikaura" was a staunch little craft, and took us
safe into port. Panama has been described so often
that I need not enlarge upon my stay, which was only
of a few hours' duration. Suffice it to say that a party
of us breakfasted at the grand hotel, and that both
fare and surroundings were of such a nature as to
make us forget the filthy street by which we had
reached its cool and pleasant shade.

Hurrying over my meal, I wandered alone through the
streets and into the churches, one of which would not
be used as a drill shed at home, with its tawdry images
falling to pieces, its tinsel and paint torn and effaced,
and its very pavement full of holes. The chief cathe-
dral was in better repair, and on approaching the grand
altar I saw a fellow-passenger, Monsignor the Catholic

Bishop of Wellington, deeply engaged at his devotions. Thinking that he might be ignorant of the near approach of the hour at which we were to cross the Isthmus, and might possibly miss his train, and perhaps his passage, too, by the "Tasmania," which was to take us from Aspinwall, the other side of the Isthmus, I sent an acolyte to inform him that a gentleman would be glad to speak to him, and, on his assenting, ascended the imposing steps to the high altar, and whispered the information relative to the approaching departure of the "Kaikaura" passengers across the Isthmus. He professed himself much obliged, and shortly after left. Those few hours in the train through a dismal fœtid swamp, with a deadly-green rankness of purple vegetation crowding up to the very lines, alligators basking in the sun on rotten logs half in and half out of the slimy morasses, turtle lazily waddling through the stagnant pea-soup-colored water as we shot past them at the magnificent pace of 30 miles an hour, and villages now and then struggling into view, formed of a few wretched huts, and more miserable inhabitants, with a general odour suggestive of yellow fever, cholera and plague, are like a strange and unpleasant story that one scarcely likes to recall ; and when we arrived at Colon we found little else but strong rum and dirty streets to make the retrospect less gloomy.

There was a revolution going on, of course, while we were in the place, as they say there always is ; but beyond a few ugly boys lounging about the wharves with old-fashioned pieces, some with fixed bayonets and some without, I saw no appearance of warfare whatever.

As Kingston has been described by many poetic and descriptive pens, I will merely *en passant* refer to the strange picture that might be painted of negro girls coaling there or at St. Thomas's. Some hundreds of ebon beauties (?) carrying each a basket of coals on her head, and crowding one behind another up the planks to the ship in a never-ending string, form one of the most strangely picturesque sights I have ever beheld, and would form a fit subject for Mr. Frith's appreciative pencil.

St. Thomas, with its pretty harbour, on the shores of which were visible the wrecks thrown up by the late tidal wave, and the lively colours of its buildings, will be always a picture pleasant to recall to memory of my homeward voyage. We were very fortunate in our weather, and in not having more illness on board, although we had as many as twenty-seven cases of shagras fever at one time ; and we were happily almost free from yellow fever, only four cases having occurred, and those just after leaving St. Thomas. The fact of yellow fever being on board was not generally known till we were in the Channel, and all danger of its spreading out of the question. At St. Domingo, on the night we touched there, we saw the fire of the rebels on the heights above the town of Jacmel, and heard from the post-office authorities, who had been on shore, that the consuls were in considerable alarm as to what steps

to take for their own protection.   Very soon after
leaving this, I was once more in London !

W. II. WILLIAMS, PRINTER, ELIZABETH STREET, MELBOURNE.